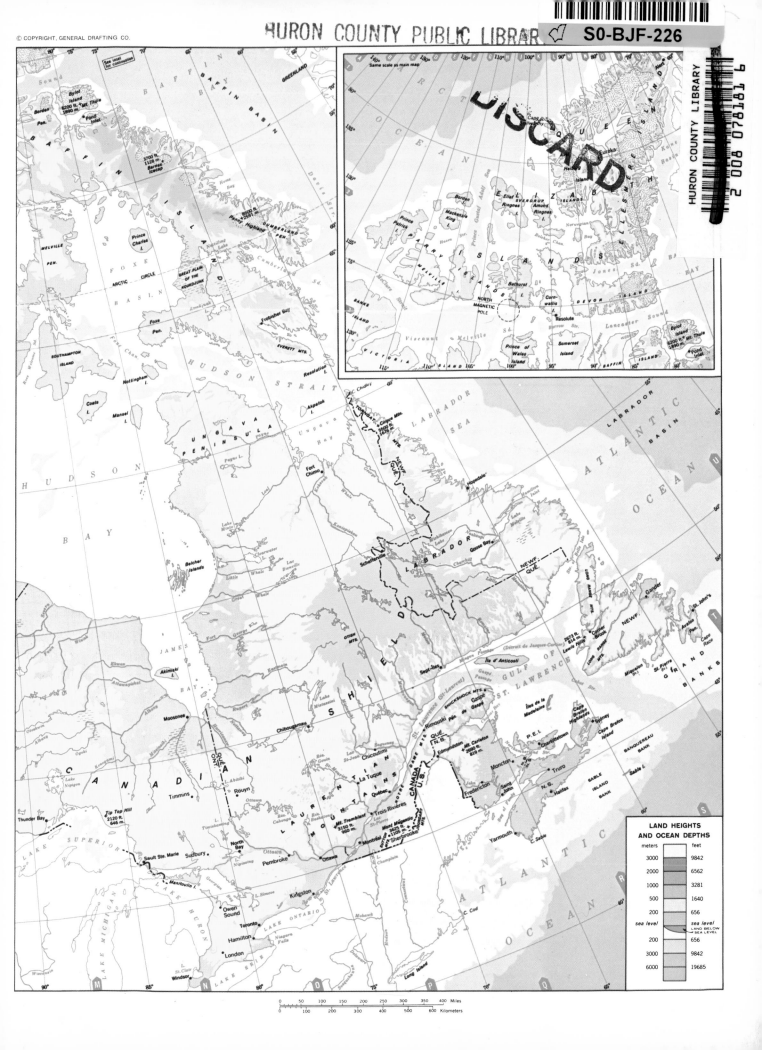

LAND HEIGHTS
AND OCEAN DEPTHS

meters		feet
3000		9842
2000		6562
1000		3281
500		1640
200		656
sea level		sea level
		LAND BELOW SEA LEVEL
200		656
3000		9842
6000		19685

0 50 100 150 200 250 300 350 400 Miles

0 100 200 300 400 500 600 Kilometers

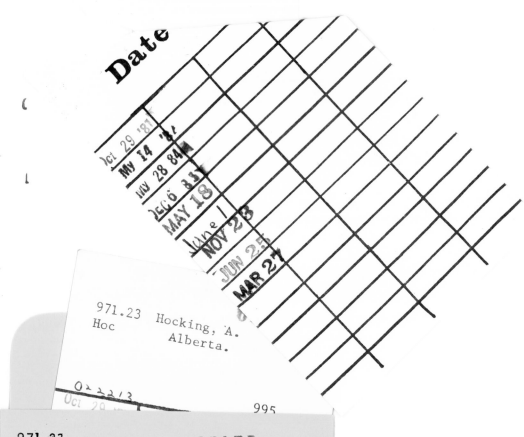

Alberta
ANTHONY HOCKING

Publisher: John Rae

Managing Editor: Robin Brass

Manuscript Editor: Jocelyn Van Huyse

Production Supervisor: Lynda Rhodes

Graphics: Pirjo Selistemagi

Cover: Brian F. Reynolds

◻THE CANADA SERIES

McGRAW-HILL RYERSON LIMITED

Toronto   Montreal   New York   St. Louis   San Francisco
Auckland   Bogotá   Guatemala   Hamburg   Johannesburg
Lisbon   London   Madrid   Mexico   New Delhi   Panama
Paris   San Juan   São Paulo   Singapore   Sydney   Tokyo

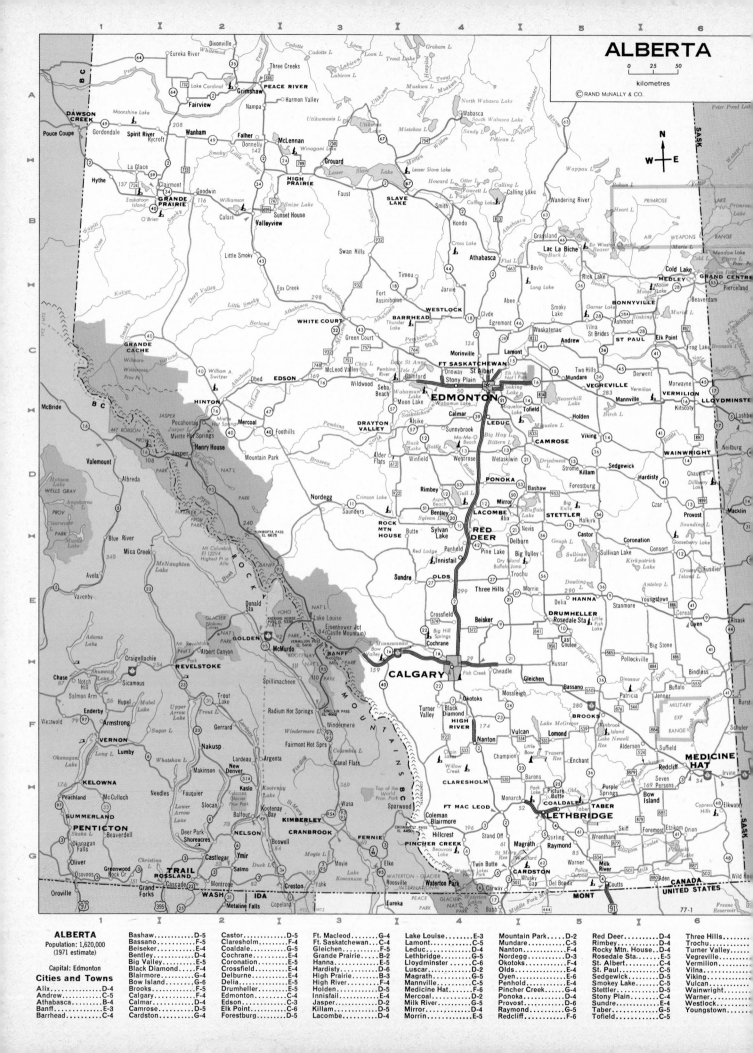

ALBERTA

0 25 50
kilometres

©RAND McNALLY & CO.

77-1

CONTENTS

ALBERTA

Alberta is the princess province. Like one of its most famous landmarks, Lake Louise, it is named after a daughter of Queen Victoria. Princess Louise Caroline Alberta was married to the Marquess of Lorne, who was governor-general of Canada from 1878 to 1883.

The princess's name was first applied to a district of the old North West Territories and was retained when Alberta became a province in 1905. At the time its population was tiny, consisting of scattered handfuls of white pioneers and the remnants of Indian tribes ravaged by white men's diseases.

The situation changed dramatically as colonists arrived to take up free land. Some were from other parts of Canada, but most were from Europe and the United States. By the 1920s nearly all the farmland with any potential was occupied, and there were settlers from the Cypress Hills to the Peace river.

In its earliest days, Alberta's fortunes were built on the fur trade. Later, ranchers, mine operators, and wheat farmers made their contributions. All these have been overshadowed by the industries developed to exploit Alberta's oil and natural gas, which have made it Canada's most prosperous province.

Alberta's wealth continues to attract new settlers as in the pioneer era, but today most of them head for the cities rather than the countryside. Calgary is the fastest-growing city in Canada, and Edmonton is close on its heels. The growing population provides new markets for Alberta's farmers and manufacturers.

On top of their material success, today's Albertans are advancing rapidly in their cultural and recreational life. Their performing arts are the best supported in Canada, and their sports representatives have done them proud all over the world. Perhaps best of all, sunny Alberta offers much of Canada's finest scenery within an easy drive of its major cities.

The glorious reflections of Lake Louise in Banff National Park, one of Canada's leading tourist attractions. Like Alberta itself, the lake is named after one of Queen Victoria's daughters.

THE LANDFORMS

Canada's three most dominant landforms are the Precambrian Shield of the north, the flat plains of the interior, and the high mountain ranges of the west. Alberta is the only province in which all three are represented.

'Precambrian' is the geological term applied to rocks formed earlier than about 600 million years ago, and therefore lacking skeletal fossils by which they can be dated. In Canada, such rocks form a vast, shield-like plate that provides the bedrock core of the North American continent.

In Alberta, only in the north-east is the Precambrian Shield exposed on the surface. It is characterized by a jumble of rock formations that are probably the roots of ancient mountain systems. From the north-east the shield dips below layers of sediment formed on the beds of ancient seas and fresh-water swamps.

The sediments lie wedged above the shield as it plunges to the west and south. The oldest that appear on the surface were laid down in the Devonian

period, between 350 million and 400 million years ago. Tertiary strata in the south-west and south-east were deposited up to 60 million years ago.

Between the Devonian and Tertiary formations are those laid down in the Cretaceous period, between 60 million and 135 million years ago. These are the formations that underlie all but a fraction of Alberta's plains. The sediments are soft, and in places river valleys have worn deep canyons that expose the sediments in cross-section.

Some of these canyons are so rough and barren that early settlers called them 'badlands.' The most famous are in the valley of the Red Deer river, and there are more in the Oldman valley. River valleys created in the Tertiary formations are less stark and are more closely integrated with the agricultural land that adjoins them.

The Cretaceous period saw the creation of the third of Alberta's distinctive landforms, the Rocky mountains. Sediments laid down in earlier periods were pushed up, responding to pressures in the earth's crust. In places the surface

High above the treeline, snow highlights the even strata that belie the Rockies' rugged profile.

rocks were folded, in places they were broken and made to overlap like shingles on a roof.

Before the mountain-building started, the sediments were covered by a shallow sea. As soon as they were exposed above the surface, the forces of erosion set to work. The sediments accumulated over hundreds of millions of years were sculpted into the spectacular formations that today attract visitors from all over the world.

In Alberta's south-west corner, near Waterton Lakes National Park, the mountains rise from the plains with no warning. Farther north there is a buffer zone of rugged foothills. Mountains, foothills, and plains all bear the marks of the one influence that affected the whole province, the passage of the glaciers.

Four separate sheets of ice swept over Alberta during the Ice Age. Some mountain peaks escaped, but otherwise

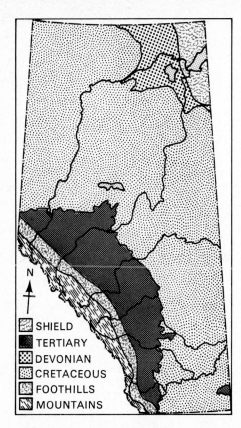

In Alberta's north-east corner is a segment of the Precambrian Shield, and in the west are the Foothills (Cretaceous/Jurassic/Triassic) and Rocky mountains (Paleozoic/Precambrian). Between them are the plains.

Legend for map:
- SHIELD
- TERTIARY
- DEVONIAN
- CRETACEOUS
- FOOTHILLS
- MOUNTAINS

the whole province was submerged. Rocks were worn down, valleys were gouged out, and quantities of debris were dumped on the plains as till or moraines. In the north, snake-like eskers formed of sand mark the route of rivers that flowed within the ice.

The last of the glaciers retreated from Alberta 10 000 years ago, but traces of it survive in the mountains. One example is the Columbia icefield between Banff and Jasper, which straddles Alberta's boundary with British Columbia. The icefield is the source of several glaciers, one of them the Athabasca.

Icefields are formed by compacting snow. Surface ice is hard and breaks easily, but deeper down the ice is plastic and can flow in response to gravity. The Athabasca glacier travels about five kilometres from the icefield and drops 550 m until it dissolves in a lake.

The Athabasca glacier, a frozen river flowing from the Columbia icefield. On each side and at the toe are chaotic accumulations of rock thrown out by the glacier as its ice disintegrates.

Dinosaur Bones

In 1884 the geologist J. B. Tyrrell recovered a fossilized dinosaur head from the Horseshoe canyon near Drumheller. Since then, many complete skeletons have been located. The Red Deer badlands have become famous as one of the world's richest sources of dinosaur remains.

No doubt there are dinosaur fossils concealed beneath the surface all over Alberta's plains, but only in eroded river valleys are they accessible. The oldest were laid down fairly late in the age of reptiles, about 80 million years ago, and the youngest are of dinosaurs that died at the end of the Cretaceous period.

Most of Alberta's dinosaurs lived in tropical swamps that bordered North America's inland sea, though some were marine creatures. The commonest remains are of amphibious 'duck-billed' dinosaurs, creatures that were about 10 m long and walked on their hind legs. One species is known as the Edmontosaurus.

Alberta's dinosaurs were of many shapes and sizes. Most were plant-eaters, but there were also flesh-eaters that preyed on their unfortunate neighbours. The largest flesh-eaters had powerful hind legs, sharp teeth, and claws on their feet, and one of the most fearsome species is known as the Albertosaurus.

At the Dinosaur provincial park near Brooks, fossilized remains are displayed where they were discovered. This is the skeleton of a duck-billed dinosaur, an amphibious creature that walked on its hind legs.

Dinosaur remains from the Drumheller region and elsewhere are displayed in museums all over the world, but the Dinosaur provincial park north-east of Brooks contains several skeletons left where they were found. Each rainfall in the park washes more sediment from the valley walls, and new bones come to light.

TREES AND GRASSES

Arid grassland covers much of southern Alberta, and trackless forests blanket most of the north. Between the two is a wide zone of parkland where trembling aspens battle grasses for command of the soil.

The trembling aspen is a species of poplar, a deciduous tree with flat-stemmed leaves that quiver in every breeze. Each aspen originates with a wind-blown seed, but once established it can clone itself by sending up suckers from its roots. In time, a whole grove of aspens forms from a single plant.

To the north, aspens share the forest with spruces and other conifers. In the parkland, they must compete with deep-rooted fescues and other tough grasses. In an even contest aspens hold their own, but in the past they were often defeated by fire. Grasses could recover more quickly, and the aspens' advantage was lost.

Since the arrival of settlers, prairie fires have been rare. Steadily the aspen

Forest carpets the mountains of north-west Alberta in the Hinton region. In summer, the Alberta Forest Service keeps a sharp lookout for fires.

The southern plains are for the most part bare of trees, but two-thirds of Alberta is forested.

is consolidating its hold on the parkland, and the range of the northern forest is being extended to the south. Meanwhile, the parkland shrinks further as more grass is ploughed under for agriculture, and in the south-east native grasses are in danger of over-grazing and invasion of sagebrush.

Outside the grassland and parkland, Alberta's vegetation falls into three forest zones. The largest zone covers most of the north and is part of the belt of boreal forest that circles the northern hemisphere. Aspens and white birches are prominent in the south, and white spruce, tamarack, and black spruce become dominant farther north.

Balsam fir and jack pine are found in the eastern regions of the boreal forest, and alpine fir and lodgepole pine are in the west. These two species are also found in the subalpine forest zone of the western uplands. At the higher elevation, the chief difference is that white spruce gives way to its near relative, Engelmann spruce.

Even higher than the subalpine zone, stunted conifers brave winter

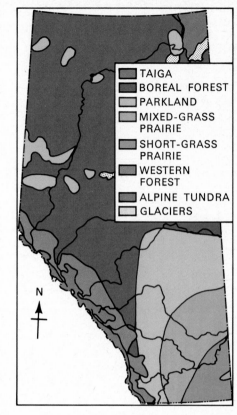

- TAIGA
- BOREAL FOREST
- PARKLAND
- MIXED-GRASS PRAIRIE
- SHORT-GRASS PRAIRIE
- WESTERN FOREST
- ALPINE TUNDRA
- GLACIERS

N

winds and extend to the treeline. Scattered stands of black spruce, alpine larch, and other species are interspersed with lichens and a carpet of flowering plants that briefly bloom in celebration of summer.

The Rivers

Two of Alberta's river systems carry 75 per cent of the water that reaches the prairie region to the east, most of it meltwater from the Rockies' spring runoff. One system feeds the North Saskatchewan river, and the other drains into the South Saskatchewan.

Both systems are valuable to Alberta as well as to its eastern neighbours, but the more crucial is the South Saskatchewan. Several of the rivers that feed it are tapped to irrigate farmland that would otherwise be short of water. However, Alberta is committed to allowing much of the water to flow unimpeded.

Only a small portion of the South Saskatchewan is within Alberta. It begins where the Oldman and Bow rivers come together, and carries the same water under a different name. The Bow's source is Bow Lake, between Banff and Jasper. The Oldman rises farther south and is fed by the Belly and St. Mary rivers.

Another element of the South Saskatchewan system is the Red Deer river. Like the others it rises in the Rockies, and has carved a spectacular

valley through the sediments of the plains. The Red Deer snakes southwards and crosses Alberta's eastern boundary before it combines with the South Saskatchewan and courses to the east.

A height of land separates the South Saskatchewan from its sister of the north. The North Saskatchewan rises in the Rockies not far from the source of the Bow. It travels north-east to Edmonton, then east towards its rendezvous with the South Saskatchewan. Their water eventually empties into Lake Winnipeg in Manitoba, from where it is carried to Hudson Bay.

The Bow river courses through Banff National Park on its way to Calgary and the east. In the background is Mount Rundle.

The rivers of northern Alberta are part of the Mackenzie system, which drains into the Arctic ocean. The river that travels farthest is the Athabasca, fed by the Athabasca glacier in the Rockies yet emptying into Lake Athabasca in the north. The Peace river has the same destination but rises in British Columbia. Lake Athabasca drains into the Slave river, which heads north to Great Slave Lake in the Northwest Territories.

The Climate

Alberta is Canada's sunniest province. The mountain ranges of British Columbia intercept air moving in from the Pacific and drain it of moisture. The Rockies' eastern slopes are in a rain-shadow, and Alberta's skies are clear on most days of the year.

Of course, sunshine is not always accompanied by mild temperatures. Summers can be hot, but winters are long and cold. The mountains that block the path of Pacific air also channel cold air from the north during winter and hot air from the south-west during summer.

Periodically, 'chinook' winds from the west manage to cross the Rockies, and warm air descends on the foothills and other parts of southern Alberta. The wind can raise temperatures by many degrees within minutes, to the extent that snow melts and the grass is exposed.

The growing season in southern Alberta lasts about 120 days and decreases towards the north. There, the shorter growing season is offset by longer days and lower altitude. Wheat is grown as far north as the Peace river country, where the local growing season is extended through the influence of the Peace and Athabasca rivers.

The Rockies intercept moist air sweeping inland from the Pacific, and leave Alberta's skies free of clouds.

Public Archives of Canada C-403

Equipped with horses but not yet possessing guns, Indians of the plains chase bison over the sheer drop of a buffalo jump. A watercolour by A. J. Miller, 1867.

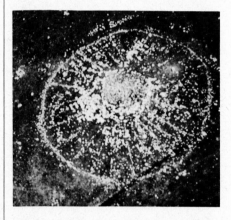

Alberta holds a number of 'medicine wheels,' enigmatic circles of stones whose purpose is not understood.

Though embellished with modern additions, pictographs in Writing-on-Stone provincial park are an exciting record of Alberta's past.

Medicine Wheels

The Indians who lived in Alberta before history began left fascinating glimpses of their culture. Stone projectile points, pictographs and petroglyphs, pottery, and teepee rings help archaeologists to analyze the lifestyles of centuries ago.

Alberta's archaeologists have identified some 10 000 prehistoric sites in the province, ranging from temporary campsites marked by rings of teepee stones to sophisticated buffalo kill sites in use for centuries. The oldest site is near Taber, where the remains of a child were uncovered. Geological evidence suggests that the bones could date back more than 40 000 years.

There is more positive evidence of man's presence from about 12 000 years ago, as hunters moved into what is now Alberta in the wake of the retreating glaciers. From then until quite recent times, peoples of the plains and foothills lived a deeply spiritual existence within the limits set by nature.

Some of the most dramatic prehistoric sites were buffalo jumps, used by Indians to stampede herds of buffalo over cliff-edges. Head-Smashed-In jump in the Porcupine Hills was the largest in Canada and was used from about 3600 B.C. until about 1850 A.D. Other famous kill sites include the Old Woman jump and the Dry Island jump south-east of Red Deer.

Buffalo were often featured in the pictographs and petroglyphs that Indians painted or scratched on stone. Some of the designs celebrated great events, some had religious significance. Writing-in-Stone provincial park in Alberta's south includes 58 separate rock art sites, a greater concentration than anywhere else in Canada.

Alberta's most controversial prehistoric sites are the so-called medicine wheels, stone circles which some authorities say were used as astronomical observatories. Several of the wheels have a rim and radiating spokes, some have a central cairn, and some consist of radiating spokes without a rim.

Supporters of the observatory theory say that the 'spokes' were lines of sight to the position of the sun on significant days. Their opponents deny that the wheels were so scientific, and say they were religious or ceremonial. Whichever side is right, the wheels remain an enigma and pose fascinating questions about prehistoric man in North America.

GUNS AND HORSES

Long before white men penetrated Western Canada, their influence preceded them. Trade goods like copper cooking pots, iron axeheads, and steel sewing needles reached the Blackfoot and other tribes of the prairies at the dawn of the eighteenth century.

The goods were supplied by the English of the Hudson's Bay Company and the French of the St. Lawrence. Cree traders acted as middlemen in voyaging west to make contact with the Blackfoot and other tribes. They exchanged their trade goods for skins of beaver, wolf, and other creatures, and also for pemmican rations.

The Crees had one great advantage over the Indians of the prairies — white men's guns. They were able to extend not only their trading influence, but their political influence too. Tribes of the prairies were driven westwards from their traditional hunting grounds, towards the Shoshoni who were as great a threat as the Crees.

The Shoshoni had horses, the descendants of animals introduced by Spanish adventurers far to the south. Quickly spreading to the north, the horses — 'large dogs,' as tribes like the Peigans described them on first view — offered immense advantages to those who possessed them.

So it was that in the region of Alberta the two most significant influences introduced to North America by white men came together. Accounts survive of a battle that took place about 1730, when for the first time Crees armed with guns confronted mounted Shoshoni armed with bows and arrows. The Crees triumphed.

After being squeezed between the Crees and Shoshoni and after being decimated by smallpox, which was another contribution of the Spanish, the prairie tribes rallied. The Blackfoot, Bloods, and Peigans acquired both guns and horses through small skirmishes with their oppressors.

Horses were a status symbol and the more a man acquired the greater his wealth and influence became. More practically, horses and guns transformed the buffalo hunt and enabled war parties to travel long distances. Within two decades the three tribes became the most powerful force on the western prairies.

A Blackfoot chief and his subordinates, as painted by Paul Kane after his travels in the west in the 1850s.

WHITE EXPLORERS

In 1754 a small party of Cree traders left York Factory on the south coast of Hudson Bay, heading for the lands of the Blackfoot far to the west. With them was a white man, Anthony Henday of the Hudson's Bay Company.

Henday was English, a former smuggler from the Isle of Wight. The chief purpose of his trip was to find out why the supply of furs from the west was dwindling in both quality and quantity. For months he and the Crees travelled across the prairies, until in October they crossed the Red Deer river.

The party was intercepted by a small band of Blackfoot and escorted to the main camp. The encounter was the first between a white man and the most powerful tribe of the plains. After inspecting Henday and listening to what he had to say, the Blackfoot broke up their camp and dispersed to the foothills for the winter.

For the Crees, the trip was routine. They travelled farther west to wait for spring, and then began their long journey back to Hudson Bay. At a prominent river crossing they met the Blackfoot again, this time ready to trade

the furs they had trapped during the winter.

Pelts from the Blackfoot filled more than 70 canoes, and Henday noted that the average quality was high. On the long journey eastwards he discovered why so few were reaching Hudson Bay. The Crees stopped at two French trading posts far down the Saskatchewan river, and exchanged most of their best furs for brandy.

There was little the Hudson's Bay Company could do to combat its French rivals, apart from sending more men to the interior. In 1759 Henday went again, this time accompanied by Joseph Smith. They visited not the Blackfoot but their allies, the Bloods, and persuaded some to accompany them all the way to York Factory.

So began a long association between the company and the Bloods, matching an older arrangement with the Chipewyans of the Athabasca region farther north. When the French posts on the Saskatchewan were abandoned during the Seven Years War, the British were left unchallenged and retained their monopoly for more than a decade.

Then English-speaking traders from Montreal entered the arena, supported

With the badlands of the Red Deer valley in the background, Indians of the plains display some of the fine beadwork that has turned ceremonial dress into an art form. Their ancestors would have worn similar clothing in the days of the explorers.

by French-Canadian voyageurs with long experience of the fur trade. Determined to outflank the Hudson's Bay Company, they ventured far into the interior to make contact with the Indians, and built trading posts in the west as the French had done.

Understanding the threat, the Hudson's Bay men took steps to shadow them. Two by two, a long line of trading posts appeared along the Saskatchewan, attracting Indians from both north and south. From the posts individual traders travelled north and west to learn Indians' languages and trade with them on their own ground.

The most successful of these individual traders was an American, Peter Pond, who set out to seduce the Chipewyans away from the Hudson's Bay Company. A long expedition in 1778 carried Pond and a party of voyageurs to the Methy portage, a route that took them beyond the Churchill river system and into Athabasca country.

Sixty kilometres from the mouth of the Athabasca, Pond built the first white man's residence in what is now Alberta. It was to be his base for more than a decade, as he and his associates reaped a rich harvest of furs from the Chipewyans and their neighbours. In 1784 they built a second post on the site of Fort McMurray.

From discussions with the Indians, Pond was convinced that the long-sought 'western sea' was close at hand — certainly much closer than Montreal. He dreamed of leading an expedition to find it, and turned in vain to his employers in Montreal to give him financial support. At one point he even approached the American Congress.

Pond never did launch his expedition, and was forced to return to the east after a brawl in which a rival trader was killed. However, he did communicate his dream to the man who took his place, Alexander Mackenzie. It was Mackenzie who ordered the building of Fort Chipewyan in 1788, and who set out from there in 1789 to explore the river that bears his name.

Like Pond, Mackenzie was em-

Public Archives of Canada C-15251

ployed by the North West Company, a loose grouping of Montreal traders who had pooled their resources to make their operations more efficient. In the Athabasca country, they had a near monopoly, for the Hudson's Bay Company was making no effort to challenge them.

Farther south it was a different story. As before, Hudson's Bay men were wintering with Indian bands, earning their respect and hopefully their loyalty. Among those who wintered with

Fort Chipewyan (right) on Lake Athabasca, for long the most important fur-trading post in the north, as painted by George Back in the 1820s.

the Peigans was the young David Thompson, later to make his name as the explorer of the Columbia river and the greatest surveyor of the west.

In the days of the fur trade, the Peace river was a major transport route. Today it is spanned by the Dunvegan suspension bridge, the only one of its kind in the province.

TRADE PATTERNS

Between them, the firms comprising Montreal's 'Nor'Westers' controlled a large number of trading posts on the Saskatchewan river system and in the Athabasca country. In 1792 they built Fort George south-east of the site of St. Paul, their first post in central Alberta.

The Nor'Westers were locked into a power struggle with the Hudson's Bay Company. Whenever they built a post on the Saskatchewan system, the company built a rival post close by. No sooner was Fort George in place than the Englishmen erected Buckingham House beside it.

Wood Crees, Peigans, and other Indians came to the two new posts to trade, and young servants of the Hudson's Bay Company accompanied them to their wintering grounds, exploring the land and learning of their ways. In 1795 the Nor'Westers built a new post farther west, Augustus House, near the site of Fort Saskatchewan.

Once more the Hudson's Bay Company was quick to follow suit, and a second post was built on the site. It was named Edmonton House, after an estate near London owned by the company's deputy governor. Edmonton House's location was changed several times in later years, and not until 1830 did it find a permanent home.

The trade of the region around the two newest posts was especially rewarding, and in later years the two companies and a rival, the short-lived XY Company, built several more of them. Meanwhile, in 1799 the Nor'Westers built Rocky Mountain House far to the south-west, and the Hudson's Bay Company shadowed it by building Acton House.

In spite of their keen rivalry, relations between the traders in the field were friendly. The twinned posts offered them companionship during the long months of winter and support when things went wrong. There were furs enough for all, and both companies became increasingly efficient.

After the turn of the century, however, relations deteriorated. The Napoleonic wars created difficulties for both companies, and in many areas furs were in short supply. Previously defensive, the Hudson's Bay Company became aggressive, and in 1815 sent a large expedition to challenge the Nor'Westers in the Peace river country.

The Hudson's Bay men built Fort

The Missionaries

Beginning in the 1840s, Protestant and Roman Catholic missionaries laboured to convert Alberta's Indians to Christianity. The first to arrive was a Methodist, Rev. Robert Rundle. Based at Fort Edmonton, Rundle had notable success with the Stoneys of the Banff region and the Crees of the north.

The first Roman Catholic was Father J. B. Thibault from St. Boniface on the Red river, who reached Edmonton House in 1842. Thibault stayed in the west for ten years and was succeeded by another priest from St. Boniface, the famous Father Albert Lacombe. In 1861 Lacombe found St. Albert, near Edmonton, as a home for wandering Métis — the descendants of white traders and voyageurs and their Indian wives.

Rev. George McDougall, the greatest of the early Methodists, arrived in the west in 1863 and soon founded Victoria mission near Pakan. As years passed, many more missionaries entered the region, and several Anglicans and Roman Catholics worked in the Peace river country. Besides making converts, the missionaries founded Alberta's first schools and first agricultural colonies.

Father Albert Lacombe, the pioneer Roman Catholic missionary who founded St. Albert as a haven for wandering Métis.

An intriguing view of Rocky Mountain House, one of the early fur-trading posts. It was sketched by Jean l'Heureux of the Hudson's Bay Company in 1873.

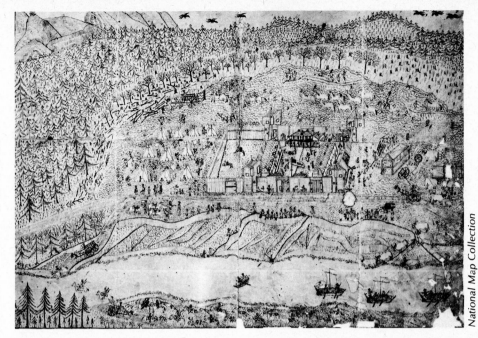

Wedderburn on Lake Athabasca, close to Fort Chipewyan. That winter they ran short of food, and Nor'Westers who could have helped them preferred to let them starve. Forced to go hunting as winter arrived, a number of Hudson's Bay men died of exposure while trying to make their way back to Lake Athabasca.

In spite of the tragedy, Fort Wedderburn proved more than a match for Fort Chipewyan. There and elsewhere, the Hudson's Bay Company steadily gained the upper hand over the Nor'Westers, and in 1821 the two companies were amalgamated. Throughout the west, twin forts were consolidated and names disappeared from the map.

In what is now Alberta, the amalgamation left Edmonton House and Rocky Mountain House as the key posts in the central region, and Fort Chipewyan and Fort Dunvegan in control of the north. Efforts to establish posts in the south were frustrated by the Blackfoot, who wanted the region to themselves.

Of all these posts, the most significant was Edmonton House, which became the distribution centre for the whole of the western prairies. Each October, convoys of York boats arrived from Norway House north of Lake Winnipeg, bringing supplies and trade goods despatched from Hudson Bay.

Some of the cargo was carried on to Rocky Mountain House up the river. More was packed on horses to be carried to Fort Assiniboine, about 100 km to the north-west. There, it was transferred to boats for shipment down the Athabasca river and across country to the Peace river.

At all the posts, Indians arrived to trade furs in both fall and spring, and at Edmonton House and Rocky Mountain House many offered pemmican too. Company servants at the smaller posts despatched the furs to Edmonton in time for the York boat convoy that left for Norway House in May. With the convoy on its way, Edmonton House settled down to a quiet summer.

Edmonton House as it appeared in 1867. The site of the post is now part of the grounds of Alberta's legislative building.

Deep in Indian country, Fort Whoop-Up, near the site of Lethbridge, became notorious for its trade in whisky. The Mounties reached the fort at the end of their march of 1874, but they found only one man inside.

Mounted police inspect traders' carts, perhaps on the Whoop-Up trail from Fort Benton, Montana. The police were searching for contraband whisky.

LAW AND ORDER

Under a royal charter granted in 1670, the Hudson's Bay Company held legally exclusive rights to the whole of 'Rupert's Land,' the vast area drained by rivers that emptied into Hudson Bay. In 1869 the company transferred its rights to the Canadian government in exchange for cash and land.

Not the least reason for the transfer was the threat of American occupation. As if to underline the danger, in the same year several parties of American traders crossed the 49th parallel to establish posts out of reach of their own authorities. Among the goods they offered were strong whisky and repeating rifles.

American traders had been dealing with the Blackfoot and other Indians for many years, but their 'whisky forts' were a new initiative. Before long, posts like Forts Whoop-Up, Standoff, and Slide-Out were attracting large numbers of Indians prepared to trade all they possessed for the white man's fire-water.

Word of the whisky forts reached the Canadian government in Ottawa, which seemed to regret the loss of customs dues as much as the corruption of the Indians. However, no action was taken until 1873, when a party of Americans massacred innocent Assiniboines whom they accused of stealing horses. The Canadian parliament passed legislation authorizing the formation of a force of mounted police.

Men were recruited and trained, and in July 1874, 300 police organized in six troops rode west from Fort Dufferin on the Red river. Their goal was Fort Whoop-Up, the most notorious of the whisky forts, and they were to put a stop to the whisky trade and set up customs posts.

At Roche Percée in what is now Saskatchewan, A troop branched north-west to head for Edmonton House, where they were to establish a police post. The remainder continued west until they came to the junction of the Little Bow and Belly rivers, where they expected to locate Fort Whoop-Up.

No fort was to be found. Provisions were running low and the animals in the party were exhausted, so the whole force travelled south to the Sweetgrass hills. The senior officers proceeded to Fort Benton in Montana to purchase supplies and ask for directions. There they recruited a halfbreed guide, Jerry Potts.

The season was drawing on, so two of the five troops were sent north-east to establish a police headquarters on the Swan river in what is now Manitoba. Potts guided the others to the whisky fort, which was deserted except for one man. The troops rode farther west and built Fort Macleod on the Oldman river.

In the next year the troop based at Edmonton House built Fort Saskatchewan a few kilometres downstream. One of the troops from Fort Macleod built Fort Brisebois at the junction of the Bow and Elbow rivers. The post was later renamed Fort Calgary after the boyhood home of the force's assistant commissioner.

Spread over such an enormous area, the North West Mounted Police were thin on the ground. They had little option but to attend to what had to be done as individuals, and it became the tradition for police to work alone or in pairs, no matter what the odds against them.

The bravery of the police quickly impressed Indians and white men alike. Wearing bright red jackets that linked them with soldiers of the queen, in a matter of two years they introduced white men's law and order to a land where previously only might had prevailed.

Public Archives of Canada C-13070

Blackfoot Confederacy

When the NWMP entered the west, the once-great Blackfoot Confederacy was in decline. Laid low by smallpox and influenza and with their buffalo in short supply because of overhunting, the tribes turned to white men's whisky for consolation.

Indian treaties cover all of Alberta. Treaty No. 4 was signed in 1874, No. 6 in 1876, No. 7 in 1877, No. 8 in 1899, and No. 10 in 1906.

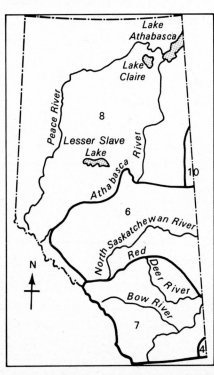

The Bloods were the largest tribe in the confederacy, but the police found that Crowfoot of the Blackfoot was the most co-operative leader. Crowfoot accepted the NWMP as a necessary antidote to the American whisky traders, and became the chief intermediary between the police and other tribes in the confederacy.

The Canadian government wanted to conclude treaties with the western Indians as a prelude to settlement, and expected the police to pave the way. Under these treaties the Indians would relinquish their lands in exchange for cash payments, guaranteed reserves, and various other benefits, including education and necessary supplies.

Treaty No. 6, involving the Crees of southern Alberta, was signed in 1874. The tribes of the Blackfoot Confederacy were invited to Fort Macleod to negotiate Treaty No. 7, but Crowfoot insisted that any meeting should take place at Blackfoot Crossing. This was agreed, and Indians and white men assembled there in September 1877.

The police had assumed that Crowfoot would be able to speak for the whole confederacy, but that was not the case. Crowfoot could make no decision without consulting Red Crow of the Bloods, who did not arrive until four days later. When at last Red Crow was present, the Blood chief graciously

Four years after signing Treaty No. 7, chiefs of the Blackfoot Confederacy reconvened to meet Canada's governor-general, the Marquess of Lorne. A sketch by Sydney Hall.

allowed Crowfoot to represent him.

So it was that on Crowfoot's recommendation, the Bloods, Blackfoot, Peigans, and Sarcees signed Treaty No. 7. So did the Siouan-speaking Stoneys, their neighbours in the mountains. Four years later the same peoples assembled again to meet the Marquess of Lorne, Canada's governor-general, when the terms of their agreement were confirmed.

Crowfoot, chief of the Blackfoot, persuaded his fellow chiefs to accept the rule of white men.

15

THE RAILROADS

At the dawn of the 1880s there were only three white settlements of any size in Alberta — Forts Macleod, Calgary, and Edmonton. The three were connected by a northern extension of the old Whoop-Up Trail from Fort Benton, Montana, which had once served the whisky trade.

The Whoop-Up Trail had been the settlements' chief link with the world outside, rivalled only by the North Saskatchewan river route. Then a stage-coach service began operating between Edmonton and Fort Qu'Appelle in Saskatchewan, by way of Battleford and Prince Albert.

In 1880 it looked as if the stage-coach route would soon be redundant. After years of planning, the Canadian Pacific Railway was to be laid across the continent. Its route was to pass Edmonton, avoiding the arid region of the southern prairies and crossing the Rocky Mountains through the Yellow-head Pass.

Then the Canadian government changed its mind. Fearing attack from the United States, it decided to reroute the line closer to the border, so that troops could be rushed in to defend it. The new route passed far to the south of Edmonton, and instead touched Fort Calgary.

Construction of the railroad's western section began in Winnipeg in 1881 and continued through 1882. Grading teams and track-laying gangs raced to

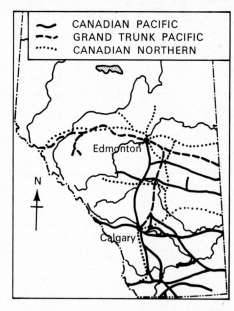

Alberta's railroads, c. 1914. By that time three transcontinental systems were in competition. Later, the Grand Trunk Pacific and Canadian Northern were absorbed by Canadian National Railways.

lay an average of five kilometres of track each day, and by May 1883 they had entered what is now Alberta.

At the site of Medicine Hat the construction crews built a temporary wooden bridge across the South Saskatchewan river. The Hat itself was no more than a tent town. The railroad sped past, and a sternwheeler was launched on the river to pull loaded coal barges from new mines on the site of Lethbridge.

The construction crews' next goal was Calgary, about 290 km away. In

Public Archives of Canada PA-38622

Building a trellis bridge on the Grand Trunk Pacific railway west of Edmonton, about 1910.

Track-laying crews at work on the Calgary and Edmonton line built in 1890.

Alberta Provincial Archives

spite of altercations with the Blackfoot, who saw their old hunting grounds invaded, the distance was achieved in two months. Like The Hat, Calgary consisted largely of tents, but soon permanent buildings were erected.

The railroad followed the course of the Bow river, leaving the flatlands and entering the foothills, until at last it reached the mountains. Banff and Lake Louise were opened to the tourist traffic that has made them world famous, and the railroad entered Kicking Horse Pass and British Columbia beyond.

So it was that the first railroad was laid across Alberta in a matter of eight months. There was no immediate rush of settlers, for most of the early homesteaders preferred lands in the eastern prairies. However, Calgary thrived in response to the new line and quickly eclipsed both Edmonton and Fort Macleod.

Not until 1890 did the CPR build a spur line connecting Calgary with Edmonton. Even then it stopped short of the North Saskatchewan river, meaning

that Edmontonians had to cross the river to catch a train. In 1892 a line was built from Calgary to Fort Macleod, and after 1897 a line from Medicine Hat to Lethbridge was extended through the Crowsnest Pass.

During these years the CPR had a monopoly of almost all freight traffic into and out of Alberta, but it was broken in 1905. In that year a second

Main street, Lethbridge, in 1884. False storefronts and the dirt road were typical of pioneer townships of the Albertan frontier.

transcontinental railroad, the Canadian Northern, reached Edmonton from Winnipeg. The Canadian Northern Railroad and yet another rival, the Grand Trunk Pacific, were later extended to the west coast.

Northwest Rebellion

Most events of the Northwest Rebellion of 1885 occurred in what is now Saskatchewan, but the most horrific took place in Alberta. A party of Crees entered the hamlet of Frog Lake and butchered nine whites, among them two priests.

The Crees were led by Big Bear, though his war chief, Wandering Spirit, was responsible for the massacre. News of the event quickly travelled across Canada and was taken as proof that the whole of the west was about to erupt. Already an expeditionary force was on its way from Eastern Canada, and the whites of Alberta prepared to defend themselves.

'Home guards' were organized in each centre, watching the movements of both Indians and Métis. As it turned out there was no more trouble, but a rancher of the Calgary area recruited 150 cowboys and others as the Alberta Field Force, and led them in pursuit of the Crees involved in the massacre.

The field force rode to Edmonton,

then headed east to Fort Pitt in Saskatchewan. The men took part in several inconclusive skirmishes with the Crees, but not until the main expedition joined in were the Crees defeated. One by one they surrendered, and eight were eventually

hanged. The Alberta Field Force returned home, and the Northwest Rebellion was at an end.

The Frog Lake massacre of 1885, in which Crees of Big Bear's band killed nine whites, including two priests.

Public Archives of Canada C-190

HOMESTEADING

In spite of the arrival of the CPR, Alberta's first party of homesteaders arrived not from the east but from the south. A wagon train of Mormons travelled north from Utah in 1887, and settled in the region of Cardston in the far south-west.

The 40 settlers of the original party were soon joined by others of their faith. Some had extensive experience of dryland farming, and to improve their land they devised an irrigation system of canals and ditches. It was the forerunner of the irrigation systems that are so important to southern Alberta's agriculture today.

The first homesteaders to arrive from the east were German Catholics, who settled east of Medicine Hat in 1889. Unfortunately their crops died because the region was too dry. Within two years they moved north to the parkland belt, settling in the woodlands east of Fort Saskatchewan.

By that time nearly the whole of the prairie region had been surveyed and was ready for settlers. Survey posts marked out a checkerboard of square townships, each divided into 36 sections. The sections were sub-divided into quarter-sections, each containing about 70 ha of land.

Many of the even-numbered sections were reserved for railroad com-

panies and colonization societies, but most odd-numbered sections were offered as free land. To claim it, settlers paid a registration fee of $10 and undertook to improve it and remain on it for three years.

More German Catholics, French-speaking colonists, Ontarians, Ukrainians, and Norwegians from the Dakotas reached Alberta in the early 1890s. However, settlement proceeded only slowly until 1897. Then the Canadian government sent agents all over the United States and Europe to recruit immigrants, and the CPR contributed to a major publicity drive.

Train after train delivered settlers to Alberta from the east, and many more

The Ranches

Ranching in Alberta started almost by accident. In 1877 an American drove 14 cows, 10 calves, and a bull from Montana to Fort Macleod, probably hoping to sell them. Somehow they became the property of a Constable Whitney of the NWMP, who, when winter approached, turned them loose on the prairie.

Next spring, Whitney rode out to see if any of his cattle had survived. To his surprise, all were intact and all the cows had calves. With a precedent set,

in 1878 a Montana rancher drove up a herd of 1000 head to graze by the Highwood river.

During the 1800s several more herds were introduced by the same route. One of the largest belonged to a Quebec senator, M. H. Cochrane, and arrived in 1881 and 1882. The herds were delivered by skilled American cowboys from Montana, Wyoming, and other states, and many of them remained in Canada and built the western legacy that survives to the present day.

By 1886 there were nearly 50

ranches in Alberta, several of them carrying tens of thousands of animals. A dry summer was followed by an early winter with heavy snow and unusually low temperatures. By the time it was over, 40 per cent of the cattle were dead. From then on, more attention was paid to cattle's winter needs.

A ranch in the Rockies, painted by Edward Roper. Some ranches raised horses, some cattle, some sheep, and a few raised all three.

Public Archives of Canada

arrived by wagon from the United States. Between 1895 and 1901 the population doubled, and between 1901 and 1906 it doubled again (to 150 000). Most of the new arrivals intended to farm, but some went to the larger settlements or to mines or the forests.

Most of the early homesteads were located in a great crescent with its back to the mountains, curving from Medicine Hat in the south to Lloydminster in the north. Later arrivals settled in the drier region east of the crescent, or in the south-west or the Peace river valley.

As homesteading spread, it quickly encroached on territory once controlled by Alberta's great ranches. Before settlers arrived, the ranchers had been able to lease large areas of the western prairies from the government at nominal rates. Now the range was being fenced, and its grass was being put to the plough.

Most of Alberta's settlers arrived by train, but this party of Americans brought covered wagons. Southern Alberta retains strong links with the states south of the border.

The Province

In 1905 Canada's parliament passed the Saskatchewan Act and the Alberta Act, creating two new provinces from the vast area of the Northwest Territories. Both extended from the 49th parallel to the 60th and were divided by the fourth meridian, which passed through the middle of Lloydminster.

At Sir Wilfrid Laurier's side when the bills were passed was Frank Oliver of Edmonton, appointed minister of the interior when Clifford Sifton resigned. Largely through Oliver's influence, Edmonton was named Alberta's capital 'unless and until the Lieutenant-Governor of the said province otherwise directs.'

The first provincial election was held later in 1905, and the Liberals, led by A. C. Rutherford, won 23 out of 25 seats. Edmonton's supporters soon thwarted suggestions that the provincial capital should be relocated in Calgary, Red Deer, or even Banff, and plans for a legislative building in Edmonton were approved.

Edmonton and Calgary had been rivals since the time when the CPR route was changed, and each campaigned hard for supremacy. Calgary was larger and more prosperous, but Edmonton had the government and before long became the educational capital. The University of Alberta was founded in 1907 and was soon in operation on the south bank of the North Saskatchewan.

The opening of Alberta's first legislature in 1906. At first the assembly sat in temporary accomodation in Edmonton, because its permanent home was not yet ready.

National Photography Collection PA-29112

SOCIAL CREDIT

Until 1921 Alberta's politics were organized on traditional party lines and were dominated by Liberals. Gradually Albertans came to suspect that they were being manipulated by Eastern Canada and took steps to make sure it would not happen again.

The initiative was taken by an agricultural organization, the United Farmers of Alberta. Angered by Eastern Canada's domination of both capital and markets, the farmers decided to oppose the Liberals in the provincial election of 1921. To their surprise, at

William Aberhart's Social Crediters were elected to power on their promise of dividends to consumers to stimulate spending. Here Aberhart signs forms requisitioning the dividends, but they were later disallowed.

their first attempt they won a resounding victory.

Installed as Alberta's government, the farmers set out to help Alberta by helping themselves. One of their early initiatives was to support the creation of the farmer-owned Alberta Wheat Pool in 1923, involving almost the whole membership of the U.F.A. and a slap in the face for the great grain merchants of Winnipeg.

With few lapses, fortune smiled on Alberta for the rest of the decade. Farms and mines flourished, communities expanded and prospered, and standards of living steadily improved. Then came the stock market crash of 1929, and like the rest of the continent Alberta was thrown into confusion.

Alberta's farmers wrestled with the money problem like governments everywhere, but were no more successful in finding answers. The wealth acquired during the years of prosperity was being swiftly eroded, and in some desperation the farmers turned to a Calgary high school principal, William Aberhart.

For many years Aberhart had doubled as a weekend radio evangelist and had won a large following throughout southern Alberta. Concerned by the worsening economy like everyone else, he had begun using his radio talks to propound radical economic theories devised by Maj. C. H. Douglas, an Englishman.

Douglas's idea was that for an economy to function efficiently, the state had to play a central part in controlling the monetary system. He proposed that to prevent inflation, the state should set a fair price for all goods, and that to stimulate spending, it should pay out a dividend to all consumers.

The dividend was to be based on the total wealth of the state, and the consumer was supposed to inject it into the economy by buying goods. This would encourage production and trigger more job creation, and so contribute to the

An Albertan, R. B. Bennett of Calgary, had the misfortune of being prime minister of Canada during the Depression years. Farmers too poor to buy gasoline yoked horses to their automobiles and named the vehicles 'Bennett buggies' in protest of government policies.

prosperity of all. Douglas described his theory as 'social credit.'

Aberhart brought an evangelist's fervour to Douglas's message, though it was later claimed that he never understood it properly. However, his listeners were impressed when he told them that their 'social credit' would amount to $25 a head per month — in the values of the day, a small fortune.

At the request of a number of U.F.A. locals, in 1934 the government agreed to consult Aberhart about the idea. When nothing came of the meeting, Aberhart announced the creation of a Social Credit party that would contest the next election. It was called in 1935, and Social Credit candidates were fielded in every riding.

The election sparked great interest throughout the province, with good reason. The results showed that the Social Crediters had won 56 of the 63 seats, while not one of the U.F.A. candidates was returned. Aberhart became premier, and Major Douglas himself arrived in Edmonton to advise him.

Not one of the Social Crediters had had previous experience of legislation, but that did not prevent them from embarking on an ambitious legislative program. To their frustration, they were never given a chance to experiment with Douglas's economic ideas. Their economic enactments were overturned by the courts or disallowed by Ottawa.

Fortunately, the economic situation was already on the mend when the Social Crediters took office. A more pressing problem was worsening drought, which affected the whole province but particularly the dryland areas of the east. Impoverished and despairing, many farmers were forced to give up their land and move elsewhere.

Again, the drought problem solved itself after 1937. In 1939 World War II broke out, and many of the unemployed escaped their difficulties by joining up. The Social Crediters were re-elected in the next year, though with a decreased majority, and when Aberhart died in 1943 he was succeeded by his able young lieutenant, E. C. Manning.

Turner Valley

Fossil fuels have been important in Alberta since the early days. CPR locomotives burned coal mined near Lethbridge and in the Crowsnest Pass. Natural gas found under Medicine Hat in the 1890s was used to provide cheap lighting and heating.

Pioneer frontiersmen noticed oil seepages in Alberta in the heyday of the fur trade, and there was a minor oil strike in the Waterton Lakes area in the 1890s. Then a former miner from Ontario, W.S. Heron, noticed an oil seepage on a farm near Turner Valley south of Calgary. He bought the farm and acquired its mineral rights.

Heron formed a company and raised capital, then sent in a drilling team. In May 1914 the team struck oil at 828 m. News of the find hit Calgary like a bombshell, and a score of exploration companies were floated. Shares briskly escalated in value as they changed hands in streetside stock markets.

The oil boom subsided when World War I was declared. However, interest revived in the 1920s and hit a peak when crude oil was discovered in 1936. The Turner Valley oilfield was the first of any significance to be discovered in the British Empire, and Calgary was 'the oil capital of Canada' from the beginning.

The Turner Valley oilfield in 1930, the strike that established Calgary as the oil capital of Alberta.

Scenery is one of Alberta's most valuable resources, and tourism is a major industry. One of the attractions is Spirit Island in Maligne Lake, Jasper National Park.

THE ECONOMY

Until 1947 Alberta's economy depended chiefly on cattle and grain, with substantial support from coal, forest products, and oil from Turner Valley. Then oil was discovered at Leduc, less than 30 km south of Edmonton.

The oil industry had been looking for resources outside Turner Valley for many years, but the Leduc strike was its first major success. By the end of 1947 there were 23 producing wells in the new field. In 1948 wildcat drilling revealed oil at Woodbend west of Edmonton, and also at Redwater to the north.

Suddenly Edmonton was nearly ringed by oilfields, far richer than Calgary's had been. Yet Calgary profited more from the new discoveries, chiefly because it was the focus of American investment in Alberta. Existing oil companies preferred to remain in Calgary rather than relocate in Edmonton, and new concerns joined them there.

For years, it seemed that Alberta swarmed with oilmen. Surveyors were everywhere, and the landscape was dotted with exploration rigs. New oilfields were discovered in a dozen locations, the most important of them in 1953 at Pembina, west of Edmonton. The others were in central Alberta and in the Peace river country.

Frequently crews drilling for oil struck natural gas instead or otherwise discovered gas associated with oil. Soon the gas was recognized as a major resource on its own, and a grid of pipelines was built to carry it to other provinces. There were six major gasfields in southern Alberta and more than a score of lesser ones.

No doubt substantial deposits of conventional crude oil and natural gas remain to be discovered, but the oil industry's interest now includes another

Winter and summer, drilling crews search for new resources of Alberta's 'black gold.' This rig is positioned near Rocky Mountain House.

Packing potatoes at a plant near Edmonton. The provincial government is pledged to expand the food processing industry, aiming to lessen Alberta's reliance on petroleum products.

resource. Alberta holds vast quantities of sand impregnated with oil, notably those those of the Athabasca region in the north-east which lie close to the surface.

Already two large recovery plants are treating oil sands excavated near Fort McMurray, and there are plans to build more of them. Three other oil sands deposits are deeper, and researchers are developing ways to exploit them. Even conservative estimates suggest that the oil sands will provide petroleum for centuries to come.

Petroleum products have made Alberta the most prosperous of Canada's provinces, and all sectors of the economy have benefited. Not only Edmonton and Calgary, but Red Deer, Lethbridge, Medicine Hat, and other communities have expanded rapidly. Alberta's population has risen spectacularly as Canadians from other provinces have flooded in.

The spread of urban areas is taking its toll of farmland, but Alberta's agriculture remains prominent. Cattle, sheep, and hogs make the province a front-runner in livestock production, and Alberta's grain harvest is second only to Saskatchewan's. In the south, intensive irrigation allows farmers to produce specialty crops and vegetables.

In the past, much of Alberta's agricultural production left the province unprocessed, but that has changed. The provincial government has deliberately promoted the local food processing industry, trying to make the economy less dependent on hydrocarbons. Even so, the growing petrochemical industry looks even more promising.

After fossil fuels and the soil, Alberta's third most valuable resource is its scenery. Tourists have been visiting Alberta since the Canadian Pacific was laid through the Rockies, but tourism as a major industry had its start in the 1950s. Now it provides considerable revenue all year round.

National parks in the Rockies and

Grain elevators at Champion, north of Lethbridge. The province is Canada's second largest producer of grain crops after Saskatchewan.

the annual Calgary Stampede are Alberta's leading tourist attractions, but the provincial government encourages visitors to sample others. High on its list of suggestions are the Peace river country, the lakeland of the north-east, and the fascinating badlands of the Red Deer valley.

Alberta's wealth has given it considerable clout as a financial centre, and both its major cities have profited. Calgary's strength rests on the oil industry. Edmonton depends partly on the provincial government and partly on its role as chief distribution centre for vast areas of Canada's north.

Grain Growing

Barley was cultivated by traders at Fort Dunvegan on the Peace river as early as 1809, and later in the century missionaries showed Alberta's Indians how to grow wheat. Then the first commercial grain farm in Alberta was established at St. Albert near Edmonton in 1876.

Today, tens of thousands of Alberta's farmers are involved in growing grain, often in conjunction with livestock operations. Wheat is the most significant crop, followed by barley, oats, rapeseed, rye, and flax. Alberta is Canada's largest producer of barley and oats and second largest producer of wheat and rapeseed.

The typical grain farm in Alberta covers 300 to 500 ha and is owned and operated by the farmer and his family. It is usually equipped with a tractor or two to pull tillage implements, a swather to lay the crop flat at harvest time, a combine to thresh the grain, and probably a large truck.

The grain farmer's year starts soon after the spring thaw, when the snow has gone and the soil is soft enough to be worked. He uses a cultivator to turn over the soil and prepare the seed bed, and a seed drill or disc to sow his seed.

Franklin gulls take advantage of tillage operations on a farm in the Peace river district. The area is a major producer of grain crops, particularly wheat, barley, and oats.

Later in the spring the growing crop is sprayed with herbicides to control weeds.

The grain should be ready for harvesting late in August or early in September. In the south-east, conditions are so dry that crops can be cut and threshed by a combine in a single operation. Elsewhere, they are first cut by a swather and laid out on the stubble to dry.

After a few days in the sun and the wind, the grain can be gathered by the combine and threshed. It is off-loaded into a truck and carried to a granary on the farm, or direct to a country elevator. There it is graded and stored until required for shipment to a terminal elevator, probably on the west coast.

Country elevators are owned by a variety of concerns which act as agents of the Canadian Wheat Board. The largest of them is the Alberta Wheat Pool, a co-operative formed in 1923. It serves farmers throughout Alberta and in parts of British Columbia, too.

AGRICULTURE

Before the turn of the century, Alberta's cattlemen had nearly all the range to themselves. Then homesteaders arrived to break sod, clear trees, and grow grain. Many of today's farmers have the best of both worlds, raising both crops and livestock.

In all, some 20 million hectares of the province are classified as agricultural land, 11 million of them cultivated. Conditions vary widely from region to region, depending on soil, climate, and topography. The least promising region is in the south-east, where drought and high winds frequently recur.

A British expedition led by Capt. John Palliser visited the south-east in 1857 and reported it was unfit for settlement. Later generations scorned the advice, and early in this century homesteaders cleared the land and sowed their seed. Until the 1920s they were successful, but then began a long nightmare of frustrated hopes and failed crops.

In the dirty thirties, eroded topsoil was blown off the land in clouds, and

Some areas of Alberta's farmland are best suited for raising cattle or grain crops, but most are utilized for mixed farming.

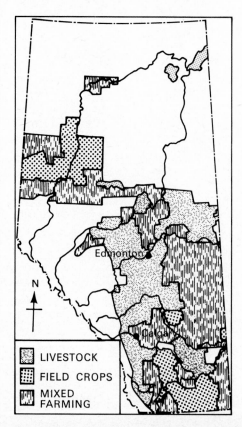

LIVESTOCK

FIELD CROPS

MIXED FARMING

Alberta holds one-third of all the sheep in Canada, but even so the sheep population is much smaller than in the days of the great sheep ranches.

dust storms buried fences and half-submerged homesteads. Destitute families abandoned their land and headed north to the Peace river valley to start afresh. Only later were conservation techniques introduced, so that today farms thrive again.

West and north of 'Palliser's triangle' is an arc of dark brown soil extending from the Lethbridge region to the area south of Lloydminster. There, the growing season is shorter than in the south-east, but rainfall is heavier and summer temperatures are cooler so there is less danger of drought.

The black soils of the parkland belt are wedged between the foothills in the west and the Precambrian Shield to the north. The region contains much of Alberta's most fertile land. To the north-west is the Peace river valley, where the growing season is shortest of all but the summer days are the longest.

All these regions support both crops and livestock. Particularly in the south, sophisticated irrigation schemes mean that farmers can grow specialty crops including sugar beets, vegetables, and corn. Forage crops also benefit. Near Medicine Hat, natural gas is used to heat greenhouses and crops are grown through winter.

Forage and some grain crops are grown to support livestock, not only beef cattle but also hogs and sheep. Alberta's sheep population is smaller than in the days of the great ranches, but even so the province holds one-third of all the sheep in Canada. Specialist hog farms are intensive indoor operations relying on rapid turnover.

Dairy farms are concentrated around Calgary and Edmonton, within easy reach of their chief markets. More than half of what they produce is processed as butter and other dairy products. The Peace river region is said to produce Canada's finest honey, a result of its

long hours of summer sunshine accompanied by relatively cool temperatures.

In the past, a large proportion of Alberta's beef, pork, grain, honey, and other products went to other provinces,

especially Quebec. Increasingly, the province is turning to new markets around the Pacific rim. Extra processing capacity within Alberta means that value is added to products before they leave.

Long hours of sunshine and cool temperatures help bees of the Peace river region to produce Canada's finest honey.

RANCHING

Grain crops make important contributions, but beef cattle are the true specialty of Alberta's farmers. Cow-calf operators produce calves and yearlings for the commercial market, and feedlots fatten them for the packing plant.

The cow-calf rancher's year begins in early spring when his calves are born, quite possibly during a blizzard. Most older cows can look after themselves, but the rancher and his hands patrol the herd to help those in difficulty. Besides, they watch for weak calves, drying them off and feeding them vitamins to build up their strength.

When the calves are about four months old, they must be branded and vaccinated against various diseases. On most ranches they are herded into a corral, roped, and wrestled to the ground. On some they are funneled through chutes. In both cases a red-hot branding iron burns the ranch's symbol into their flanks.

Sometimes the calves are dehorned, and bull calves not required for breeding are castrated. That turns them into steers, to be fattened for sale to feedlots. With branding over, both cows and calves return to pasture for the rest of the summer, and by fall the calves have been weaned.

Fall is the season of the round-up, when the calves are separated from their

Young steers in a feedlot, where they are introduced to a high energy ration that fattens them for slaughter.

mothers. Many of the steers will be sent for auction, then shipped to feedlots on the prairies, in Ontario, or in the United States. On some ranches the steers will be held back over the winter, then sold in spring or summer when they may command better prices.

Most of the mothers will be bred again, but those with poor records will be culled from the herd and auctioned for slaughter. During winter the breeding herd is left out in the open, but the cows are checked regularly to make sure they are healthy. Their feed is hay, silage, or grain grown on the ranch during the summer.

At the feedlot, the young steers are slowly introduced to a high energy ration, also based on hay, silage, and grain. Confined in pounds and fed several times a day, they rapidly gain in weight. At about 500 kg most of the gain is in fat or 'finish,' and the feedlot operator watches for the right moment to offer his cattle on the market.

The biggest feedlots are automated, and one in Brooks has room for up to 40 000 head. Most are much more

A cattle auction at the Edmonton stockyards. Buyers normally offer bids by the pound, and the purchase price is calculated by multiplying the successful bid and the animal's weight.

Breeding Programs

Before World War I, nearly all Alberta's cattle were descended from Texas Longhorns brought in from Montana. Later, ranchers introduced British breeds like Herefords, Aberdeen Angus, and Shorthorns.

Today, Herefords make up the bulk of Alberta's commercial herd, but in many cases they are being crossbred with exotic breeds from continental Europe. Exotics like Charolais, Limousins, Pinzgauers, and Simmentals grow larger than the British breeds and are more efficient in converting their feed.

By breeding an exotic bull to his cows, the rancher expects to obtain calves that will produce more red meat. Some ranchers dispense with real bulls and rely on artificial insemination. Alberta has several semen-producing businesses specializing in beef and among them they offer the world's largest genetic pool.

On occasion, artificial insemination is used to fertilize outstanding cows selected for an embryo transplant. In this operation, fertilized embryos from a donor cow are transplanted to as many as 15 recipients. By this means several outstanding calves

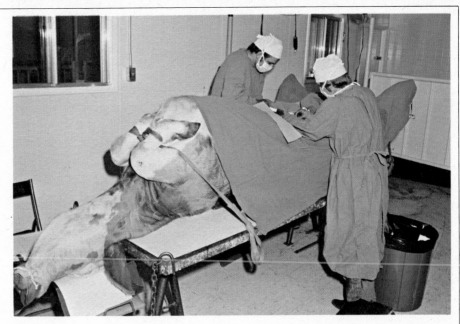

are produced from a single cow in the same year, when normally there would be only one.

A cow chosen for a transplant is injected with hormones to release a number of eggs in its next heat period. Then it is bred naturally or by artificial insemination. The recipient cows are chosen from among those coming into heat, and surgery takes place between four and six days after the donor cow was bred.

The donor is put under anaesthetic,

An ovary transplant under way in Calgary. Fertilized embryos from the donor cow are transplanted to as many as 15 recipients.

and an incision is made ahead of the udder to expose the uterus and ovaries. The fertilized eggs are removed, and those that seem to be developing normally are implanted in the recipients. In most cases, more than half of the recipients eventually produce calves.

modest and accommodate no more than a few hundred. There are about 3000 feedlots in the province, most of them part of a mixed farming operation where the farmer is utilizing surplus barley and other cereals.

More than 85 per cent of the steers finished on Alberta feedlots are sold direct to packers without going through auction rings. They are slaughtered as prime beef. Slaughter cows culled from cow-calf herds are used to make products like sausages and hamburgers. Half go through the terminal markets of Edmonton and Calgary, 40 per cent are sold in community auctions, and the remainder are sold from the ranch.

Cowboys of a ranch near Cochrane herd a small group of cows and calves across a stream during the fall roundup. When the whole herd is assembled, calves are separated from their mothers and many of them are sent for auction.

IRRIGATION

Large areas of southern Alberta have fertile soil and plenty of sunshine, but little in the way of rainfall. Local farmers compensate by irrigating their land and have transformed the region into one of the most valuable in the province.

As early as 1879, a farmer south of Calgary took water from Fish Creek to irrigate six hectares. Mormon settlers who arrived in the 1880s and 1890s irrigated land in the Cardston region and later in the area around Lethbridge. There they co-operated with the local coal-mining interests, which diverted water from the St. Mary river.

Encouraged by these schemes, the Canadian Pacific Railway set out to irrigate two enormous blocks of near-desert land adjoining its main line. The railway had acquired the land as part-payment for building its line and wanted to make the region attractive to settlers. The hope was they would use the railroad to transport their produce.

Centred on Strathmore and Brooks, the two new irrigation schemes were created between 1903 and 1914. Both were designed to draw water from several sources, notably the Bow river. Today the schemes are known as the Western and Eastern Irrigation Districts respectively, in area among the largest in Canada.

Other smaller irrigation schemes have been introduced between Waterton Lakes in the west and Medicine Hat in the east. The most elaborate is the St. Mary river system, which is fed from three major reservoirs. The water is used not only for irrigation, but also for domestic and municipal use, and for industry and recreation.

Today, irrigation schemes in Alberta are organized in 13 districts, the largest covering about 110 000 irrigable hectares and the smallest only 350. Each district is governed by a board of directors elected by the member users. Together the schemes account for more than half the irrigated land in Canada, and some 3800 farms are involved.

Water reaches the farms by means of open canals. There are three basic ways of applying it to the soil — through surface irrigation, overhead sprinklers, or pipes under the surface. The third method is not used in Alberta, but the first two are found in many variations.

Some irrigation systems are simple, some complex. Farmers match them to the crops they are growing and to the

Water Policies

Alberta's water is used not only in local irrigation districts, but in provinces to the east. Under an agreement made in the 1960s, Alberta allows at least half of the water in the Saskatchewan river system to cross the boundary with Saskatchewan.

At present Alberta suffers no loss in allowing the water to escape. Careful conservation of the Rockies' eastern slopes helps to increase spring run-off and maintain water quality, and control works downstream regulate the water's flow. Besides, much of the water delivered over the boundary is in the North Saskatchewan, which is a less crucial source than those farther south.

Even including the North Saskatchewan, the water resources of southern Alberta amount to only 20 per cent of the province's total. At present, the 80 per cent in northern Alberta is hardly used. If there is ever a water shortage in the south, it should be possible to divert water from northern rivers like the Peace and Athabasca.

Tangle Creek falls in Banff National Park, a spectacular section of the eastern slopes watershed that provides most of the water reaching Canada's prairies. Careful conservation helps to maintain the water's high quality.

efficiency they require. The simplest and cheapest of all the systems is border ditch and border dyke irrigation, when the farmer raises a control gate to release water on to sloping fields and lets gravity carry it downhill.

In another system, the farmer digs parallel furrows or corrugations in his fields, up to a metre apart. Water is released into the field or siphoned in by pipe. As it flows down the furrows, it reaches rows of crops growing between them. In some situations, water is introduced as a trickle from plastic pipes laid on the soil surface.

Sprinkler systems are more efficient than surface systems, but are also more expensive. The simplest consist of pipes that have to be moved by hand, meaning that the labour involved is considerable. Many farmers prefer systems that can move themselves, particularly side rolls and pivot arms.

In the side roll system, the irrigation pipes serve as the axle of a series of wheels spaced about 15 m apart. An engine rotates the pipes, and they drive the wheels so that the whole system moves forward at an even pace. It remains in each location for about 12 hours, and then proceeds to the next.

A disadvantage of the side roll system is that it is low off the ground. For high-growing crops, farmers prefer a pivotal system. Here the pipe is mounted on two-wheeled towers that rotate around a central pivot point. The pivot arm is designed to irrigate a quarter-section, but its rotation misses the corners.

Irrigated crops vary from district to district, but the most valuable are specialty products including sugar beets, red beets, potatoes, onions, peas, and

The farmers of southern Alberta depend heavily on the large-scale irrigation schemes that carry water to the land. Here, a farmer in the Brooks area uses plastic sheeting to cut off the flow of an open canal.

corn. In most cases these are grown around Lethbridge and Taber under contracts with processors, and they involve only a small proportion of the total area under irrigation. Most farmers concentrate on cereal and forage crops, and many use them to feed livestock including cattle and hogs.

To produce high-growing crops, farmers of the Lethbridge area use self-propelled irrigation systems that rotate around a central pivot. The system is designed to irrigate a circle that fits within a quarter-section.

THE FORESTS

Nearly two-thirds of Alberta is covered by forests. As yet only a fraction of the forests' potential is being exploited, but they are a major resource for the future. The province is making sure they are not wasted.

Before 1930, all of Alberta's natural resources were controlled by the federal government. Sawmills could purchase timber 'berths' to supply customers like the railroad companies, but most homesteaders saw timber as a nuisance. It had to be cleared before they could begin to farm.

As early as 1906 the federal government set up forest reserves in Alberta, with several aims. The first was to conserve timber supplies; the second was to prevent homesteading on unsuitable land; and the third and most important was the protection of streams by conserving timber on the upper watersheds.

The province took control of the forests in 1930. Since 1953, forest man-agement has been the responsibility of the Alberta Forest Service. This body aims to protect the forest against fire and disease, and manages the resource for the benefit of forest industries and other users.

At present, the right to cut Crown timber in Alberta depends on possession of a timber quota or a forest manage-ment agreement. Timber quotas affect smaller forest industries like sawmills and are auctioned to the highest bidders. Most involve only coniferous timber, but some include deciduous trees too.

Forest management agreements are drawn up when a company plans to construct a major facility like a pulpmill or plywood plant. There are pulpmills at Hinton and Grande Prairie, but even conservative estimates suggest that Al-berta's forest resources could support five or six more.

Under a management agreement, a company has exclusive harvesting rights over large areas of forest, on condition that timber is cut according to a plan approved by the province. The ideal is

Clearcutting in the forests of northern Alberta. The trees left standing help the harvested areas to regenerate naturally, if necessary assisted by extensive tree-planting schemes carried out by the logging company concerned or by the Alberta Forest Service.

to cut no more wood in a year than the forest can replace, allowing for destruc-tion and decay.

Most logging companies harvest timber by clearcutting, removing all the forest cover in a designated area. The technique duplicates the effect of a forest fire, which is nature's way of disposing of old, decaying forest and making way for the new. As trees are removed, fresh seeds germinate in their place.

Supporting nature's efforts, logging companies plant seedlings in the clear-cut area, and if necessary plough (scarify) the site to help them. It is a rule in Alberta that all logged-over areas must be reforested within ten years.

A Shared Resource

Besides providing forest industries with their raw materials, Alberta's woods are valuable as a living resource. They sustain wildlife, which in turn benefits trappers and hunters, they regulate the water table, and they enhance recreation.

Far from being destroyed by forest operations, wildlife habitats are often improved. Young forest growth provides succulent forage for larger animals like elk and moose. Smaller animals and birds thrive on grasses and herbs that invade the forest clearings and attract the species that prey on them.

Some forest areas, most of them in the north and on the eastern slopes, are leased to groups of ranchers as grazing lands. Cattle roam the forest pastures until the first frost, when they are rounded up and taken home. Several hectares of grazing are required for each animal.

The Athabasca country in the north is still famous for the quality of its furs. Indians, Métis, and some whites pursue beaver, muskrat, lynx, marten, and other species. Hunters hope to bag moose, elk, or white-tailed deer, or perhaps a black bear.

The roots of the forest conserve the water table and prevent soil from being washed away. Unpolluted water fills

A bulldozer piles 'slash' left from a harvesting operation for burning. Later, heavy chains are dragged across the land to open the soil for fresh seeds and seedlings.

northern lakes and supports their fish populations. In both summer and winter, Alberta's commercial fishermen use gillnets to catch whitefish, trout, pickerel, and other species.

Sport fishing is a favourite pastime in the forest regions. So is berry-gathering, for the forest produces abundant crops of blueberries, huckleberries, currants, and cranberries. But for many, it is enough to appreciate the forest for its own sake, quiet, beautiful, alive, and everlasting.

Logging companies have to do it themselves or pay the government to do it for them.

A major advantage of planned reforestation is that all the growing trees on the stand are of the same age and species and will reach maturity together. Forest conservation becomes fibre-farming, planned harvesting is made all the easier, and the continued good health of Alberta's forests is assured.

The pulpmill at Grande Prairie, one of only two major mills in the province, though the forest could support many more. Pulpwood for the mill is harvested in a large area around Grande Prairie, making sure that no more wood is cut than the forest can replace.

MINERALS

Alberta's mining industry was founded by an American, Nicholas Sheran, who crossed the border from Montana to prospect for gold. No gold did he find, but he did notice outcroppings of coal near the site of Lethbridge. In 1870 he began to mine them.

At the time, the only market for Sheran's coal was Fort Benton in Montana, about 320 km away, and he used ox-drawn wagons to haul it there. When the NWMP founded Fort Macleod in 1874, Sheran provided their winter fuel. Forts Benton and Macleod remained his best customers until he drowned in the Oldman river in 1882.

That was the year when powerful interests from Eastern Canada moved into the area to mine coal for the Canadian Pacific Railway. Led by Sir Alexander Galt, they launched a new company and founded a settlement to accommodate their miners. The settlement was later named in honour of William Lethbridge, a company executive.

Years later more coal mines were developed around Blairmore in the Crowsnest Pass. Communities like Lille, Bellefleur, Hillcrest, and Frank came into being, peopled by pick-and-shovel miners drawn from Europe. Frank and Hillcrest were to be the scenes of two of the worst disasters in Canada's history.

At Frank, the disaster was natural. In April 1903 an enormous wedge of limestone weighing tens of millions of tonnes crashed down from the mountain top, burying the railway and part of the town. At least 76 people were killed though the night shift at the mine miraculously escaped unscathed by tunnelling to higher levels.

At Hillcrest, not much more than one kilometre away, the disaster was man-made. In June 1914 a spark ignited a pocket of gas and set off a chain of explosions in the coal dust. Within moments, 189 men had died, many of them blown to pieces. Their remains were buried in a common grave nearly 100 m long.

These were high prices to pay for Crowsnest coal, but operations continued there and elsewhere. Domestic and industrial customers demanded more coal every year, and that was the position until the 1950s when a rapid decline set in. Consumers, notably the railways, were turning to oil which was cheap and in abundant supply.

The slump in coal reached its lowest point in the early 1960s, but there was an improvement when a number of producers in Alberta and British Colum-

Coal is railed to the processing plant at an underground mine in the Rockies. Most of the coal mined in the area is bituminous, destined for export to Japan.

bia signed 15-year contracts to export metallurgical coal to Japanese steelmakers. Later, Canadian markets increased as the price of oil rose and coal became competitive again.

Today, there are coal mines on the prairies, in the foothills, and in the mountains. Most are open pits mined from the surface, with the overlying soil and rock stripped away to uncover the coal beneath. Dragline excavators scoop up the coal and transfer it to large dumptrucks that carry it to a processing plant.

Some mines in Alberta, particularly those in the mountains, have to operate underground because the coal lies so far from the surface. Parallel roadways are driven into the coal seam, and the coal between the roadways is extracted in slices along the 'longwall.' As the miners advance, the worked-out space behind them is allowed to collapse.

There are four main classifications of coal, decided by its particular qualities. The hardest, anthracite, is the best domestic fuel, and is mined at Canmore near Banff. Bituminous coal is used as domestic and industrial fuel and is found in the mountains and foothills and around Lethbridge. This is the coal used in steelmaking.

Sub-bituminous coal is found in a broad zone curving from the south-east towards Edmonton and Grande Prairie. This is the coal used in thermal generating stations, often sited close to the mine that supplies them. East of it is a zone of lignite, soft brown coal that in Alberta is largely ignored.

Besides coal, Alberta produces limited quantities of salt, sodium sulphate, and peat moss, and also a number of minerals used in the construction industry, like limestone, sand, clay, and gypsum. The province is the world's largest producer of elemental sulphur from hydrocarbon sources. However, no metallic minerals are mined, though Alberta does hold several deposits of low-grade iron ore and uranium has been found near Lake Athabasca.

Back to Nature

Under legislation passed in 1963, industries interfering with Alberta lands are required to leave them as clean as they found them. Pipeline contractors, drilling crews, seismic surveyors, and others are not allowed to give up their leases until they have earned 'reclamation certificates' from government inspectors.

That amounts to reclamation after the fact. Under legislation passed in 1973, larger companies are required to plan reclamation in advance. Only after careful scrutiny of what they propose will the government allow them to proceed. The rule affects forest industries and oilsands developers, but most of all it applies to surface coal mines.

In the ordinary course of events, a surface mining operation drains soil of water, clears it of trees, ands removes the topsoil. Then dragline excavators attack the seams of coal, and a large cavity is created. The hole is filled in as the dragline advances, but the lie of the land is altered forever.

Under the reclamation law, companies have to return the land to a state equal to or better than it was in before. The piles of earth left by the dragline are graded into rolling hills and are seeded with grasses, shrubs, and trees. In some cases the reclaimed land is turned into a recreation area, in some it can be farmed.

THE OILFIELDS

Decades after the discovery of the Leduc fields in 1947, rival companies continue to scour Alberta's plains and foothills for new sources of oil and natural gas. Exploration is costly and success often depends on luck, but the potential rewards are enormous.

Oil and gas are where you find them, trapped below non-porous rock that prevents them from filtering to the surface. Geologists and geophysicists can pinpoint formations where potential traps occur, but the only way of discovering if petroleum is present is to drill through the rock and release it.

Aerial prospecting and surface investigations are both important aspects of the search for petroleum, but the most valuable tool is the seismograph. A crew sets off a miniature earthquake by exploding dynamite in a shallow hole, then uses geophone detectors to pick up echoes as sound waves hit the rock layers far below.

The geophones are arranged at set distances from the source of the explosion. By measuring the time lag between the explosion and the echoes, the seismograph crew maps the contours of the rocks. These contours may reveal a possible petroleum trap, for instance a dome in the rock or a fault where a formation is interrupted.

Depending on the results of all these surveys, and providing the company concerned has acquired the necessary mineral and surface rights, it may be worthwhile to bring in a drilling rig. The contractor's crew erects a drilling floor and a derrick above it, a hoist that on the biggest rigs towers 15 stories or even higher.

On the drilling floor is a rotary table with a square hole in the middle, connected with powerful motors beside the rig. The table rotates a square pipe known as a kelly, which is fitted to the top of a string of round pipes added one by one as the bit probes deeper into the earth.

When it is time to insert a new pipe through the hole, roughnecks in the drilling crew use the derrick to raise the kelly out of the way. When a bit has to be changed, the whole drilling string has to be pulled from the hole and dismantled in three-pipe sections, then reassembled and threaded back when the new bit is in place.

The bit normally consists of steel-toothed wheels mounted on a hollow tube. To keep it cool as it rotates, drilling 'mud' containing clay and special chemicals is pumped through the string of pipes. The mud returns to the surface outside the pipes, bringing up waste from the hole.

At the surface the mud is filtered and collected in a tank to be used again. Should the bit puncture a deposit of high-pressure oil or gas or even water, the mud acts as a fluid cork and helps to control its flow. To protect the hole, the drilling crew inserts a steel sleeve and cements it in place.

'Refinery Row' on the outskirts of Edmonton. Crude oil piped from outlying wells is broken down into its many parts.

Eight out of nine exploratory wells prove to be dry. In most cases the trap is present as the exploration team anticipated, but the petroleum has escaped or was not there in the first place. Where oil or natural gas is found, the drilling team withdraws the drill and inserts tubing topped with a valve system or pump.

The ideal oilfield produces under its own pressure. In many cases the oil is squeezed out both by water trapped below it and by natural gas trapped above, expanding to fill the space available. In the past, wells were allowed to gush and much oil went to waste, but today all phases are carefully controlled.

The tangles of pipes and valve faces installed above the surface over free-flowing wells are known as Christmas trees. As pressure lessens, it may be necessary to install a pump in the tubing at the bottom of the well. This is connected with a 'horse's head' pumping unit at the surface, powered by a motor.

On the surface a 'separator' removes impurities like natural gas, sediment, and water. Then the crude is stored ready for shipment to a refinery, where it will be broken down into its many parts. About 700 products can be made from crude oil, most of them liquids but some gases and some solids.

The first step in refining the crude is to heat it and collect vapours in a distillation tower as they condense. The chief constituents have different boiling points and their vapours cool at different levels of the tower. The method produces such substances as gasoline, kerosene, heating oil, gas oil, and lubricating oil. Some are immediately marketable, but others go forward for conversion.

In Canada as a whole just over 40 per cent of the crude oil refined is processed as transportation fuel, whether for automobiles, aircraft, ships, or locomotives. Just over 50 per cent is processed as heating fuel or as fuel to power factories. The remainder is used for non-energy purposes, such as lubricating machines or surfacing roads, or as petrochemical feedstock.

Drilling for oil, a roughneck adds a round pipe to the string probing the earth below, and reattaches the 'kelly' which transmits rotary power.

Natural Gas

Before the 1950s, most of the natural gas produced from Alberta's oilfields was burned off as waste. Some was harnessed by local communities to provide cheap energy, but there were no economic means of transporting it to communities farther away.

Then a system of pipelines was developed, carrying gas to Eastern Canada, the west coast, and the United States. The gas quickly found favour in areas not previously familiar with it, and increased its influence until today it serves about 25 per cent of all Canada's energy needs.

Eighty per cent of Canada's natural gas is produced in Alberta, much of it a by-product of oilfields but most drawn from wells that produce only natural gas. Extensive exploration has shown that the province contains much more gas than oil, and not the least of gas's attractions is that it is easy to recover.

Gas wells are drilled in the same way as oilwells, then surmounted by a Christmas tree valve system. The gas flow is directed to a processing plant where hydrocarbon liquids and moisture are removed through pressure, refrigeration, or other means. If hydrogen sulphide is present it is converted into elemental sulphur.

The processing plant also extracts liquefied petroleum gases (LPG), particularly butane and propane, which are important feedstocks of the petrochemical industry. The gas that remains is forwarded to a special plant that removes ethane, another petrochemical feedstock. That leaves purified methane, the natural gas distributed to customers in many parts of Canada and the United States.

At the gas processing plant, solid matter and moisture are removed through pressure, refrigeration, or other methods.

TAR SANDS

One day Alberta's conventional sources of oil and natural gas will be exhausted, but the province has an ace up its sleeve. The Athabascan tar sands of the north and north-east may well become the world's largest source of hydrocarbons.

The 'tar' that coats the Athabasca sands is really bitumen, a sticky, semi-solid substance that has the same constituents as oil but is structured differently. Peter Pond, the first white man in the Athabasca region, noted that Cree Indians caulked their canoes with bitumen from the banks of the Athabasca river.

Alexander Mackenzie, David Thompson, and other distinguished travellers commented on the oil sands. Early prospectors believed that the bitumen came from a pool of liquid oil beneath the surface and set out to drill

At Great Canadian Oil Sands north of Fort McMurray, a giant bucket excavator dwarfs the maintenance trucks that surround it.

for it. They discovered not oil but salt, which was later the basis of a thriving local industry.

From World War I onward, engineers looked for ways to separate the bitumen from the sand and experimented with various methods. One of the most effective was hot-water flotation, in which the sand was mixed with hot water and steam. The bitumen covering peeled off the sand and formed a surface froth that could be skimmed off.

With certain refinements, this is the recovery method favoured today. However, only recently has the rising value of oil made it economic. The first plant to exploit the bitumen for conversion into synthetic crude oil was Great Canadian Oil Sands, opened in 1967 near Fort McMurray.

A second plant, twice the size, has been built at Fort McMurray by Syn-

Huge walking draglines gouge sand coated with bitumen from the Syncrude area near Fort McMurray. The sand is conveyed to the processing plant in the distance, where the bitumen is recovered.

Heavy Crude

Petroleum scientists classify liquid crude oil as light, medium, or heavy, depending on its thickness. Most of Alberta's liquid crude is light or medium and is easily extracted and refined, but there are also vast resources of heavy crude that have been little used.

Alberta's heavy crude was first discovered in 1925, when a well was drilled near Wainwright, south-west of Lloydminster. Since then, two large reservoirs have been identified, one underlying Lloydminster and the other farther north under Cold Lake. Both deposits continue beyond the boundary with Saskatchewan.

For many years heavy crude has been extracted from the Lloydminster field not to produce energy, but to make asphalt for paving roads. Heavy oil needs sophisticated upgrading before it can be refined, and in the past this has been uneconomic. Now an upgrading plant is to be built in the Saskatchewan sector of Lloydminster.

The heavy crude at Cold Lake is even thicker than the Lloydminster deposits and was originally regarded as 'oil sand,' like the deposits at Athabasca. However, it is responding

well to the 'huff and puff' recovery process, by which steam is pumped down wells for a month at a time.

The steam heats the oil, which can then flow more easily. At the same time it puts pressure on the oil to move up the well when the steam is cut off. The well flows for two months or so,

A row of horsehead pumps sucks heavy crude from the deposits at Cold Lake, near the Saskatchewan boundary.

and then the whole cycle is repeated. At present the heavy crude is trucked to a refinery in Edmonton, but a new refinery is to be built on the spot at Cold Lake.

crude, and there are plans to develop several more. At each, the company concerned has leased areas of the sands from the Crown and must excavate its raw materials by quarrying them from open pits.

Except in the valley of the Athabasca, which cuts into them, the sands are hidden beneath substantial rock overburden and a surface layer of muskeg. Once the upper layers have been removed, giant excavators dig into the sands and transfer them to a system of conveyor belts that carries them to the processing plant.

Inside the plant the bitumen is separated from the sand by hot-water flotation and is then ready for upgrading into synthetic crude. The large molecules of bitumen are 'cracked' into smaller ones like those of naphtha and gas oil. Unwanted substances are removed, and the naphtha and gas oil are mixed to form crude.

The main body of the Athabasca oil sands covers some 23 000 km² around Fort McMurray, though large quantities are too deep below the surface to be mined in the open. There is another large deposit around Peace River and several much smaller ones in the north, all far underground.

To exploit these deeper deposits, engineers are developing new extraction methods. One possibility is the 'huff and puff' technique already being used to recover heavy crude at Cold Lake, where steam is pumped down wells to heat the oil and help it to flow.

A second technique involves 'fire flooding,' by which a well is drilled and the bitumen is deliberately set on fire. Air is pumped through a second well and fans the fire to higher temperatures. Vapours from the bitumen are pumped to the surface, where they cool and condense not as bitumen but as crude oil.

The largest deposit of tar sands is in the north-east. Others are far underground, but the heavy crude deposits of Cold Lake are being exploited.

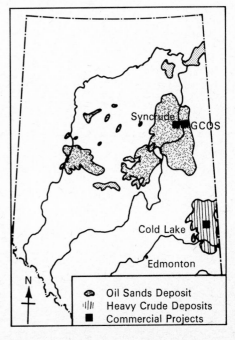

Syncrude GCOS

Cold Lake

Edmonton

N

🟤 Oil Sands Deposit
⫿⫿⫿ Heavy Crude Deposits
⬛ Commercial Projects

MANUFACTURING

From the sugar refinery in Taber to the bakeries of the Peace river country, food processing is Alberta's largest manufacturing sector. Much of what it produces is consumed locally, but increasing amounts are being exported.

Meat, particularly beef, accounts for more than half of the industry's output. Most of the large meat packing plants are located near the terminal stockyards in Calgary and Edmonton, but there are

Meat packing in a plant attached to Calgary's stockyards. All cuts are carefully inspected for grade and quality.

Petrochemicals

Alberta's oil is better known than its natural gas, but the gas is more abundant and for the moment more useful. Besides being valuable as an energy source, the gas contains hydrocarbon feedstocks used in Alberta's growing petrochemical industry.

The industry had its start in 1941, when a plant was constructed near Calgary to make ammonia from natural gas. In the 1950s, new plants were opened in Edmonton and Fort Saskatchewan, producing industrial chemicals, fertilizers, and polyethylene resins. More chemical and fertilizer plants went into production in the 1960s.

Today, these efforts are being eclipsed. With the approval of the Alberta government, a number of groups are working to extract greater benefits from natural gas before it leaves the

province. In particular, the gas is being stripped of its ethane, the basis of a major building block for a series of important chemicals.

The ethane is being extracted at four locations — Waterton, in the remote south-west; Cochrane, near Calgary; Fort Saskatchewan; and Empress, on the Saskatchewan boundary. Next it is piped to a major new complex constructed at Joffre near Red Deer, where it is heated in the presence of a catalyst and 'cracked' to produce ethylene.

A small quantity of the ethylene goes to a manufacturer of paint ingredients in Edmonton, but most is piped to a large plant in Fort Saskatchewan. There, it is converted to make a variety of chemicals used to make consumer products, among them various ethylene compounds and vinyl chloride monomer.

Ethylene not required at Fort Sas-

katchewan is piped to petrochemical plants in Sarnia, Ontario. So is surplus ethane not needed at Joffre. Most of the vinyl chloride is upgraded to polyvinyl chloride (PVC) at another plant near Fort Saskatchewan, and the PVC and ethylene products are passed on to 'downstream' manufacturers.

With raw materials so readily available, the hope is that more 'downstream' manufacturers will locate in Alberta. Some would make industrial chemicals, but the greatest potential is in plastics. There are strong markets for polyethylene products, whether low (limp) or high (rigid) density, or for polyvinyl chloride, which can be combined with additives to make everything from plastic pipes to synthetic leather.

Even before the Joffre gas ethylene plant came on stream, there were plans to build a second one alongside it. In time, the Joffre area may be filled with chemical works. Elsewhere, a consortium is planning to build a petrochemical complex near Bruderheim, making benzene from a condensate of liquefied natural gas.

According to some estimates, at present consumption levels Alberta's natural gas will last at least until 2010. Ethane and other feedstocks amount to less than five per cent of the gas produced. Even if stocks run low, the new plants can be adapted to alternative feedstocks, for instance hydrocarbons from the Athabasca oil sands.

A fertilizer plant in Fort Saskatchewan, near Edmonton. The plant utilizes by-products of the petrochemical industry.

others in Lethbridge, Red Deer, and elsewhere. Government inspectors monitor all stages of production and grade the eventual products.

Taber's sugar refinery processes sugar beets produced locally, and there are plants in the vicinity that process peas, corn, and other specialty crops. Flourmills operate in centres like Lethbridge and Medicine Hat, and there are dairies and bakeries throughout the province. Rapeseed oil and honey are processed in a number of locations.

The pulpmills of Hinton and Grande Prairie are Alberta's largest individual forest industries, and foresters say there is enough wood to support several more. At present, sawmills and other lumber manufacturers account for more than 60 per cent of total forest production.

Nickel from mines in Manitoba and Ontario is refined at Fort Saskatchewan. There are two modest steel foundries in Calgary and a larger steel-making mill in Edmonton. The capital and Camrose both hold pipe-making mills that supply steel pipe to Alberta's pipeline com-

panies.

A more impressive steel industry may be developed through the efforts of Steel Alberta, an investment corporation set up in 1976. The corporation has bought land containing iron ore in Montana and has an option on ore deposits in the Peace river country. A local steel mill would be able to smelt the ore with coal mined in Alberta.

Food processing is an important element in Alberta's economy, and the provincial government has set out to increase its range. Here, vegetable oil is refined and bottled in a plant near Edmonton.

Workers leave Edmonton steelworks at the end of their shift. As yet Alberta's steel industry is small, but it is quickly expanding in response to the needs of secondary manufacturing and the construction industry.

CONSTRUCTION

Alberta's prosperity is reflected in its construction industry even more than in the manufacturing sector. Calgary and Edmonton are expanding both upwards and outwards, and the boom is shared by communities from Lethbridge to Fort McMurray.

Fortunately for the industry, the boom is self-supporting. Continuing prosperity attracts new arrivals who re-

The site engineer and a steel rigger confer over the plans of a construction project in Edmonton. Alberta's two major cities are the fastest-growing in Canada.

quire accommodation, which helps residential construction. The new arrivals also want services, which produces a need for new commercial and institutional projects, and manufactured goods, which justifies new factories.

Until quite recent times construction projects ground to a halt during the winter months, but improved techniques help the industry to function throughout the year. This makes it all the more productive. Several local construction firms that started small have grown into industrial giants that can take on projects far outside Alberta's boundaries.

Albertan firms so excel in the specialized engineering involved in petroleum production that their technology is being exported worldwide. The en-

Workers prepare steel reinforcing before concrete is poured and their project proceeds.

gineering firms and those in other fields are supported by a growing number of industries that provide their raw materials, notably steelwork, concrete, timber products, and electrical equipment.

In all its branches, the construction industry is organized with a strong commitment to private enterprise. Projects are usually contracted on the lowest tender. In theory, outside companies have as strong a claim on them as local firms, but in practice the Albertan concerns have grown strong enough to stand up to any competition.

Compared with the situation elsewhere in Canada, Alberta's industry has a reputation for finishing projects quickly and sometimes under cost. On occasions, however, things go wrong — as when there is a strike, or if the weather does not co-operate, or if raw materials are late in arriving.

In all its activities, the construction industry depends heavily on the attitudes of the three spheres of government — federal, provincial, and municipal. Taxes may be increased, permits may be withheld, and public projects may be delayed.

In the 1960s, the federal and provincial governments reduced their support of the industry so substantially that there was a serious slump. Today, the provincial government is once more the industry's most important client, particularly through hospital and school construction.

Outside Calgary and Edmonton, the most ambitious development project in recent years has been Fort McMurray. Whole armies of workers are attracted there from other parts of Canada and Europe. Unfortunately, the great majority of them are unskilled, which means there has been an unemployment problem even when there has been a shortage of skilled workers.

Turning the surplus to its advantage, Alberta's government has organized training programs to equip the unskilled with trades. So far nearly 40 trades are represented in the program, and it is regarded as one of the most advanced of its type in North America.

Fort McMurray, sited on Alberta's tar sands, has provided thousands of jobs for construction workers both skilled and unskilled.

Architecture

The province's construction boom has produced a significant number of architectural innovations, not only in Edmonton and Calgary but in other centres too. Among them are several that have aroused international attention.

One of the most striking designs is the 'horizontal highrise' that houses the University of Lethbridge. The building stretches along the side of a coulee, overlooking the Oldman river in the valley below. Its design is in close harmony with the surrounding terrain and is best seen from the opposite side of the valley.

Among Calgary's special prides is the Devonian Gardens, an indoor park

The University of Lethbridge, a 'horizontal highrise' constructed in a coulee above the Oldman river.

above a sophisticated shopping mall. The park covers a full hectare, and includes a large number of trees and shrubs and channels with running water. The gardens have proved an attraction both for Calgary residents and for visitors, particularly during winter.

Calgary's Convention Centre and the Calgary Tower are impressive too, and so are large-scale office complexes like Calgary Place and Scotia Square. In Edmonton, the courts building and the nearby Citadel Theatre have been praised, and so have the Commonwealth Stadium and developments like the round-towered Chateau Lacombe Hotel.

TRANSPORTATION

Rivers were Alberta's first transport routes, and two of them are still being used. For 120 days a year, barges carry cargoes on the Athabasca river north of Fort McMurray, and on the Slave river between Lake Athabasca and Great Slave Lake.

The barges and the tugs that push them have a draft of less than two metres and can travel down the Mackenzie river and in the Arctic ocean beyond. Their cargoes include food, housing, and machinery, but much of their work is concerned with artificial drilling islands erected in the Beaufort sea.

At one time, the river route to the north was the only one available. Now there are sophisticated flying services, and a road and railroad reach to the Northwest Territories. River transport is less costly but not so fast, and is limited to the months of summer and fall.

The first roads in Alberta were the trails pioneered by early traders, notably the Whoop-Up trail of the south. Today, the busiest route is the highway between the two major cities. In Calgary it is known as the Edmonton trail, in Edmonton as the Calgary trail, but it provides rapid communication between the two.

Crossing the province, most traffic uses the Trans-Canada Highway in the south. The highway is routed past Calgary and Medicine Hat and through Banff National Park. An alternative is the Yellowhead route to the north, which goes by way of Edmonton and Jasper. Yet another possibility is a southern route through the Crowsnest Pass.

The chief highways run close to the main rail routes that cross Alberta. CP Rail's is in the south, linked with a complex tangle of secondary lines serving communities and grain elevators. Canadian National's is in the north, and has spread long tentacles to reach for northern resources.

The railroad system was long a sore point in Edmonton, which never forgave Canada's government for rerouting the original CPR line to Calgary. In Alberta as a whole, there is deep resentment over high rail freight rates on everything but grain, which has been carried at artificially low rates since 1897.

Most aviation in Alberta is centred on Edmonton and Calgary. Both cities have major international airports, and

Bulk trains carrying coal, potash, or wheat traverse the Rockies by means of Kicking Horse and Yellowhead passes. This is a CP Rail coal train near Banff, bound for the west coast.

Alberta's great cities are connected by an uninterrupted highway. Calgarians know it as the Edmonton Trail, and Edmontonians as the Calgary Trail.

Calgary's has direct connections with a number of cities in the United States. In Edmonton, much of the traffic uses the old municipal airport close to the city centre.

Twelve times a day in each direction, 'air buses' carry passengers between Calgary and Edmonton. Smaller aircraft converge on Edmonton from elsewhere in the province and from outside. Visitors instinctively duck as approaching flights zoom low over the downtown area, but Edmontonians are used to them.

Aviation services, road and rail transport, and river routes have all helped to make Edmonton the 'capital of the north,' not only of Alberta but of all Canada. Already a railroad connects Edmonton with Hay River in the North-west Territories, and the Mackenzie Highway's long journey to Yellowknife starts at Peace River. As these routes are extended, Edmonton's links with the north will become even closer.

Trucks play a major role in transporting agricultural produce within Alberta. Here, sugar beets are delivered to the refinery in Taber.

Bush Pilots

In the 1920s and 1930s, a group of young aviators based in Edmonton helped to unveil the resources of the north. Known as 'bush pilots,' they shepherded their fragile aircraft over vast areas of uncharted terrain and relied on ingenuity to keep out of trouble.

Many of the pioneer airmen had been fighter pilots during World War I and had learned their skills over the fields of Belgium and France. In Canada, they learned to navigate by following rivers, ferrying freight and passengers to distant locations. They also helped the RCMP, made the first aerial surveys for the mining industry, and many times flew mercy missions to avert disaster in remote communities.

A number of the bush pilots have been admitted to Canada's Aviation Hall of Fame, which is in Edmonton. Not far away is the airfield where many of them were based. Originally known as Blatchford Field, Edmonton's municipal airport was opened in 1927 and is the oldest in Canada.

PIPELINES

Oil and gas can be transported by tank trailers or rail tankers, but in most situations pipelines are safer and more efficient. There are more than 100 000 km of pipelines buried in Alberta, and they enmesh the province like a spider's web.

Laying pipelines under water poses special problems for the contractor, but a trench is dug as on dry land.

Alberta's first pipeline was built in 1912 to carry natural gas to Calgary from the Bow valley field. Several other gas lines were laid, and then came the discoveries at Leduc in 1947. Almost immediately it was decided to build a crude oil pipeline linking Alberta with Eastern Canada. Known as the Interprovincial, it was commissioned in 1950.

The Interprovincial starts at Edmonton and is under federal jurisdiction. So is the Trans-Mountain, a crude oil pipeline completed in 1953 to link

A pipeline is welded together, wrapped in insulating materials to protect it from rust and corrosion, and swung into its trench.

Edmonton with the west coast. Natural gas is collected by Alberta Gas Trunk Lines, and most of it is piped to Alberta's boundaries, where it is delivered to systems that carry it east, west, and south.

A company wanting to lay a new pipeline must survey the land, acquire the rights-of-way, and win government

When a route has been chosen and rights-of-way have been acquired, a ditching machine excavates a trench. When the pipeline is in place, the ditch is filled in again.

approval. That accomplished, construction crews grade the surface and ditching machines excavate a deep trench. In rocky terrain the trench must be blasted with dynamite.

The pipe is strung along the trench in sections, and welders connect them to form an unbroken ribbon of steel. X-ray cameras check the welds for faults, and mistakes are rectified. Then a machine wraps the pipe in asphalt, glass fibre, and felt to protect it from rust and corrosion, and it is swung into the trench.

The pipe is tested under government supervision after the trench has been filled in. Before long it is almost impossible to tell that the surface has been disturbed. Neat control valves are fenced off, and at intervals there are compressor or pumping stations, many of them operated by remote control.

Crude oil is pumped to Alberta refineries or the Interprovincial's terminal in Edmonton. The Interprovincial is sometimes used to carry other products like liquid propane and liquid butane as well. Natural gas pipelines are entirely separate from those carrying liquids. The gas is transmitted at low temperature and under high pressure, after treatment in a compressor station.

Main transmission pipelines whether for crude oil or gas have diameters of up to 100 cm, and secondary lines have diameters of less than 15 cm. Even smaller lines transmit gas or carry crude from wellhead batteries to the secondary transmission network. In many areas, plastic pipes carry natural gas to rural consumers.

All pipelines are regularly patrolled — often from the air — to make sure all is well. Operators must guard against corrosion, pipe failure, and worst of all, the danger of someone hitting the pipe when digging. Always there is a chance of a spill or even an explosion, but safety standards are high and accidents are rare.

Natural gas is pressurized and transmitted through narrow-gauge pipelines. Here, technicians test a new installation.

Electricity

Pipelines provide an integrated transportation system below the surface, and powerlines match it in the sky. An electrical grid shared by Alberta's utilities links communities from the 49th parallel to within 150 km of the Northwest Territories.

The largest of the utilities is Calgary Power, a private corporation that generates nearly 65 per cent of Alberta's electricity. The company has several hydroelectric generating plants on the Bow and North Saskatchewan river systems, and two large coal-fired plants near Edmonton.

Calgary Power's biggest customer is the City of Calgary. The utility also sells supplementary power to the City of Edmonton, which has its own generating stations, and to Lethbridge and Red Deer. The one major community to escape its influence is Medicine Hat, which supplies its own power by burning natural gas.

Central and southern Alberta are served by Calgary Power, but in the north and east, power is distributed by another private corporation, Alberta Power. The company has two large coal-fired generating plants and a number of small ones equipped with gas turbines.

CALGARY

Calgary was founded as a police post, developed as a rail junction, and has flourished as an agricultural centre. Its colourful past is fondly remembered, but its present is chiefly concerned with a phenomenon of the twentieth century — the oil and gas industry.

The industry began with the lucky discovery of the Turner Valley oilfield in 1912. From then until the 1930s, there were periodic booms and busts as Cal-garians responded to new finds in the area. Turner Valley was an education, and when the Leduc field was discovered in 1947, it was Calgarians rather than Edmontonians who rushed to take advantage.

Calgarians have retained their edge to the present. Edmonton is the geographic centre of Alberta's petroleum industry and is the operational headquarters. But Calgary is the centre of administration for oil and gas operations all over Canada and in many other

Calgary's highrise downtown core is located not far from the Bow river. All around are suburbs that sprawl towards the open prairie.

countries. Calgarian expertise is highly regarded all over the world.

Nearly 500 oil and gas exploration companies have their head offices in Calgary. Nearly 300 consulting firms are based there, and so are most of Canada's well-drilling contractors and geophysical surveyors. Nearly 400 of the

---

The American Connection

Southern Alberta has much in common with the northern United States. There is no geographic difference, for both areas are part of the plains. Indians and white men passed freely over the 49th parallel even after the international boundary was declared.

Many of Alberta's pioneer settlers were from the United States, and brought with them the attitudes of the plains. To this day, many southern Albertans feel claustrophobic in the mountains, even though they can be seen from Calgary. Plains people appreciate a landscape with distant horizons and an expanse of clear sky.

The American connection was reinforced by the oil industry. In the 1950s, Canadian investors were more interested in base metals than in oil and natural gas. That was when American corporations began investing heavily in Alberta and sent management personnel to represent their interests. The influence is still felt today.

One American tradition that has thrived in southern Alberta is a special pride in 'western hospitality.' The tradition stems from the days when trails were long and lonely, and homesteads few and scattered. Doors were left unlocked, and it was perfectly in order for strangers to make themselves at home.

Even today, Calgarians will put themselves out for visitors in ways that astonish people from other parts of Canada. In Stampede week, even the most conservative deck themselves in cowboy boots and white stetsons to join in the fun, and the good will generated by all the excitement seems to last throughout the year.

industries' service and supply companies have headquarters in Calgary, and most of the pipeline contractors also.

To service the industries' needs, Calgary has greater computer capacity than any other centre in Canada. A new phenomenon is the growth of research facilities, not least those concerned with unconventional feedstocks like the Athabasca tar sands. In all, some 70 per cent of jobs in Calgary depend directly on oil and natural gas.

Particularly since the energy crisis of the early 1970s, the population has expanded rapidly. Some of the new arrivals are from other parts of Western Canada, but most are from the east. Calgary has had to annex large areas of surrounding farmland for new residential development. Fortunately, the plains provide plenty of room.

There have been major changes in the city centre too. Oil companies like to congregate as close together as possible, and most of them are housed in a handful of major developments occupying a few downtown blocks. There, progress is upwards rather than out-

Calgary is full of parks, and Albertan sunshine encourages many to make use of them. Here a squad of young cheerleaders is put through its paces.

wards, and the skyline is rising to meet the revolving restaurant that tops the Calgary Tower.

Several downtown blocks include sophisticated shopping malls, and one contains the Devonian Gardens, Calgary's remarkable indoor park. Close by is an outdoor pedestrian mall extending six city blocks and the city's convention centre, which profits from its location so close to the mountains.

Attached to the convention centre is the home of the Glenbow-Alberta Institute, one of Canada's finest museums and art galleries. The original Glenbow Foundation was the brainchild of Eric L. Harvie of Calgary, an oilman who used his wealth to collect records and artifacts relating to Canada's Old West.

Southern Alberta's history is brought to life in Calgary's Heritage Park, a historical village portraying the region's development from the time of the pioneers. Fort Calgary is the site of the old NWMP post, and an interpretation centre explains Calgary's early history. Close by is one of Canada's finest zoos, complete with a special park containing 75 lifesize statues of dinosaurs.

The oil industry has brought Calgary wealth and prestige, but it has also helped to develop new enterprises. Local manufacturers thrive on the booming population, as do local farmers. Far from turning Calgary into a one-industry town, the oilmen are helping to diversify its economy and give it a broad base for the future.

Stamp Around Alberta

Tourism is Alberta's third largest industry, and more than half of its business comes from Albertans. Most tourists converge on the mountain parks of the Rockies, but the provincial government has been working to entice them to other regions.

For tourism purposes, the province has been divided into 14 zones. They range from the 'Gateway' and 'Chinook Country' of the south, to the 'Land of Midnight Twilight' and 'Land of the Mighty Peace' in the north. Calgary and Edmonton are zones in

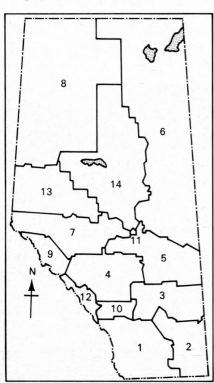

The flying saucer landing pad in St. Paul, a tongue-in-cheek project that has become a leading tourist attraction. Close by are natural gas flames at which 'little green men can warm their hands.'

their own right, as are Jasper and Banff national parks.

The government's most imaginative program used the 14 zones to the full. Every household in the province was issued with a 'holiday passport,' complete with spaces for passport stamps. The idea was that families would visit the various zones in turn and collect passport stamps as they travelled.

A family with stamps from six or more zones could claim a minted medallion from Travel Alberta, the province's tourism authority. Stamps from six zones earned a bronze medallion, stamps from ten zones earned a silver, and stamps from all 14 earned a gold.

Starting in 1978, the offer was to stand for three years. It became an instant success, not only with children but with adults too. All over the province, stamping centres were invaded both by Albertans and by outsiders who wanted to join in. The tourism industry prospered, and Albertans learned much more about each other.

Alberta's tourist zones are: 1. Chinook Country; 2. Gateway; 3. Big Country; 4. David Thompson Country; 5. Battle River; 6. Lakeland; 7. Evergreen; 8. Land of the Mighty Peace; 9. Jasper; 10. Calgary and District; 11. Edmonton; 12. Banff; 13. Game Country; 14. Land of Midnight Twilight.

COMMUNITY SPIRIT

Queen Elizabeth II toured Alberta in 1978 and was shown two remarkable sights in small towns east of Edmonton. One was the world's largest decorated egg, and the other was the world's only landing pad for flying saucers.

The egg is at Vegreville, the centre of a farming district settled by Ukrainians. At Easter, Ukrainians decorate eggs with geometric patterns to celebrate the season of new birth. The giant egg is more than 10 m tall, is mounted high on a revolving stand, and consists of scores of aluminum triangles in many colours.

The flying saucer landing pad is in St. Paul, where much of the population is French-speaking. It was built to mark Canada's centennial in 1967, and it contains a time capsule that will not be opened until 2067. Close by are three eternal flames fed by natural gas, where 'little green men can warm their hands.'

The egg and the landing pad have become tourist attractions, along with Drumheller's dinosaurs and Cardston's Mormon temple. Peace River in the north bases a flourishing tourist industry on the spectacular grave of Twelve Foot Davis, a local pioneer who made a fortune from the Cariboo goldrush in British Columbia.

Tourists bring dollars, and the whole community profits. Even more helpful, however, are new businesses and new residents. Many of Alberta's smaller communities have deliberately set out to attract new blood, putting money into face-lifts designed to show that they take themselves seriously and have confidence in their future.

At one time that future looked bleak. Most smaller communities were losing residents to the cities and were dying on their feet. Their revival began in the 1960s, and since 1975 they have been helped by a remarkable program known as Main Street Alberta. Funded by the Devonian Foundation of Calgary, the program helps communities to freshen up and regain their self-confidence.

Some towns have refurbished buildings or developed parks. Some have organized local celebrations like rodeos, bonspiels, and community picnics, old customs that had fallen into disuse. Nearly 100 towns have been involved in revival projects so far and have made

their money go further by recruiting volunteers to do most of the work.

Community spirit is strong in many of the larger towns and in smaller cities too. At Lethbridge, a service organization recreated Fort Whoop-Up. As a centennial project, the community built the now-famous Japanese Friendship Garden, an oasis of peace where kimonoed guides explain the heritage of their ancestors.

Medicine Hat's chief claim to fame is its name, one of the most curious in Canada. Various stories are told to account for it, but they are all the result of guesswork. The Hat is also famous for its natural gas and the petrochemical plants that process it, and for the Cypress Hills near by that are an island of forest in a sea of grass.

Red Deer is the halfway point between Calgary and Edmonton and is named after its river. The city began as a railroad townsite, and has long been an important distribution centre. With the opening of the petrochemical complexes in the Joffre valley, Red Deer is emerging as a business and industrial centre too.

Half of Lloydminster is in Alberta and the other half is in Saskatchewan. The provincial boundary runs down the main street. Even so, by arrangement with the two provinces, a single munici-

The Japanese Friendship Garden in Lethbridge was created to celebrate Canada's centennial in 1967. Guides of Japanese descent are on hand to explain aspects of their culture.

pal authority governs the whole city. It is named after Rev. G. E. Lloyd, the leader of the pioneers who settled the region in 1903.

The most northern city in Alberta is Grande Prairie, part of the Peace river farming district. Forest industries and oil and gas exploration contribute to the economy, and an annual attraction is Alberta's only festival of logging sports.

Populations

Statistics Canada 1976 mini-census showed that Calgary had a population of 469 917, thus overtaking Edmonton, which had 461 361 people. Other populations include the following:

Lethbridge	46 752
Medicine Hat	32 811
Red Deer	32 184
Grande Prairie	17 626
Fort McMurray	15 424

A war memorial dominates the main street of Red Deer, the city sited halfway between Calgary and Edmonton. Red Deer has become important as a manufacturing centre, not least through the ethane extraction plant built at Joffre to the east.

Jasper Avenue, Edmonton's main street. The avenue provides an unbroken link with the days when Edmonton was a fur-trading post, and today it is a corridor leading straight to the heart of the business district.

The highrise buildings in Edmonton's city centre. Not far away is the valley of the North Saskatchewan river, free of development and a playground for the city.

EDMONTON

In spite of its rapid growth and its northern location, Alberta's capital is the greenest city in Canada. Nearly 15 per cent of its area is parkland, most of it contained in a 40 km strip along the banks of the North Saskatchewan river.

The river cuts Edmonton in half, and the parkland provides spectacular set-tings for many of its important buildings. On the north bank, highrise blocks in the downtown area tower over the legislative building. To the south, the campus of the University of Alberta overlooks several of the bridges that tie the city together.

Until 1912, the north and south banks were in separate municipalities. Edmonton has grown around the old fur-trading post of the north bank, which was not torn down until 1915. Strathcona to the south had developed around the terminus of the Canadian Pacific Railway. Its citizens were not pleased to be absorbed by their larger neighbour.

Many of Strathcona's older buildings have survived, but of Edmonton's there are few traces. Fortunately the city is recreating its past in an extensive park located beside the river. The park's centrepiece is a detailed reconstruction of the old fur-trading post, and close by there are streets of buildings representing the lifestyles of 1885 and 1914.

Edmonton's one unbroken link with its early days is Jasper Avenue, Alberta's most famous thoroughfare. Once a rough trail used by Red river carts and stagecoaches, the avenue became Edmonton's main street. Today it is a corridor that leads to the heart of the business district and the elegant stores near by.

Within two blocks of Jasper Avenue is Edmonton's civic centre, like no other in North America. Its core is Winston Churchill square, a block-size open space of grass and trees. Around three sides are the city hall, central library, law courts, and municipal art gallery.

The fourth side is occupied by a complex of retail stores and offices, the Edmonton Centre. All the buildings are connected by underground walkways, which are a major advantage in winter. In time, most of central Edmonton will be accessible by these 'pedways,' which are also connected with stations on the city's light rapid transit system.

The Edmonton municipality controls the whole of the local transit service, as happens in many Canadian cities. However, it also controls local electricity supplies, water, and telephones, as well as the famous municipal airport close to the city centre. The airport is a reminder of Edmonton's long history as supplier of the north.

Culturally, Edmontonians are among Canada's keenest supporters of theatre, symphony, and opera, and ballet is gaining a foothold. The provincial museum and the Edmonton Art Gallery are major influences, and so is the University of Alberta. Standards of cuisine have been improving, as has the quality of Edmonton nightlife.

'Refinery row,' east of the city, is the most obvious evidence of Edmonton's industrial strength. Not so obvious are the petrochemical works, meat-packing plants, and other enterprises zoned out of sight, particularly as Edmonton takes pride in its clean environment and means to keep itself as pollution free as possible.

Edmonton House has been reconstructed several kilometres upstream of its original site and is the centrepiece of a notable historic park that counts among Edmonton's leading tourist attractions.

Klondike Days

In 1898 gold was discovered in the Klondike region of the Yukon, 2500 km from Edmonton. Promoters in Eastern Canada induced fortune-hunters to travel to Edmonton by train, then continue onto the goldfields by way of the 'Klondike Trail.'

Unfortunately no such trail existed, as some 2000 easterners discovered when they arrived in Edmonton. Only a handful of them ever reached the Yukon, but many liked Edmonton so much that they stayed. The community prospered, the population tripled, and Edmonton felt itself in touch with world events.

For ten days each July, Edmonton revives the heady atmosphere of the gold rush with Klondike Days, a fine excuse for dressing up and stepping out. Stores are adorned with false fronts, stagecoaches rattle along Jasper Avenue, and elegant costume garden parties are given in the grounds of the legislature.

A highlight of Klondike Days is the 'world championship' sourdough raft race, when home-made vessels flounder perilously out on the river. Those who capsize can console themselves at the blackjack tables of the Golden Garter saloon, or by panning for real gold in the Chilkoot mine on the bank.

Melodramas play to packed houses and bands march in the streets. Western hospitality is everywhere, not least in shopping malls where free sourdough breakfasts are served. Perhaps best of all, Edmonton's downtown streets are closed to traffic for a whole Sunday afternoon, and up to 200 000 Edmontonians and visitors promenade there to learn something new about their neighbours.

During Klondike Days, Edmontonians dress up in costumes like those worn in the heady days of the Yukon gold rush.

The province's legislative building stands on the banks of the North Saskatchewan river, close to the site of Edmonton House. The legislature first sat in the building in 1911, though it was not completed until the following year.

The provincial government is responsible for administering Alberta's natural resources, among them the immense tar sands deposits at Fort McMurray.

GOVERNMENT

With Edmonton confirmed as the provincial capital, Alberta's legislature had to decide where to erect a permanent building as the government's home. The obvious site was close to Edmonton House, overlooking the North Saskatchewan river.

At the time Edmonton House was still standing, and it survived until torn down in 1912 to make way for a bowling green. Meanwhile, the government approved a design for its headquarters — four wings in the shape of a cross, surmounted by a huge dome. The cornerstone was laid in 1909, and the completed structure was opened in 1912.

The building was centred on the legislative chamber, but it also housed all departments of the public service. In fact, there was room to spare. Since then, government has grown, and today departments are scattered all over Edmonton and, indeed, all over the province.

As elsewhere in Canada, the public service's function is to administer the laws passed by the legislature. Each department is set up by an act of the legislature which defines its powers and responsibilities, and each is headed by a minister who must answer to the legislature for its activities.

The biggest departments are those concerned with education, health, and social services, in that they have by far the largest budgets. Among the others are those administering agriculture, natural resources, business development, municipal affairs, highways, labour, and consumer affairs.

Alberta Culture and the Department of the Environment hold briefs to improve the quality of life in Alberta. The Energy Resources Conservation Board in Calgary monitors the petroleum and coal industries. The Treasury holds the pursestrings and balances each department's needs and aspirations against the financial resources available.

One branch of government deliberately independent of the others is the judiciary, expected to interpret the law whether federal, provincial, or municipal. In 1979 Alberta's court system was streamlined to dispose of overlapping jurisdictions and now consists of two main divisions.

The senior division is the Court of Queen's Bench, with its headquarters in the courts building in Edmonton. Queen's Bench justices sit in Edmonton, Calgary, and ten other judicial centres,

Administrations

In the past Calgarians tended to vote Conservative, while Edmontonians favoured the Liberals. At first the Liberals (L) comfortably held their own, but disaffection with Ottawa and Eastern Canada steadily eroded support for both national parties.

Instead, to their own surprise Albertans elected a home-grown party in the election of 1921. The United Farmers of Alberta (UFA) continued to govern until 1935, when they were succeeded by William Aberhart's Social Crediters (SC). In 1971 the Social Crediters were defeated by Peter Lougheed's Progressive Conservatives (PC).

Albertans have sometimes been accused of favouring 'one-man' governments, content to trust a single

| Aberhart | Manning | Strom | Lougheed |

individual with near-absolute power. Certainly that seemed to be the case with Premiers Brownlee, Aberhart, and Manning, and there are some who have seen the same trend in the administration of Peter Lougheed.

Alberta's premiers have served as follows:

A. C. Rutherford (L)	1905 — 1910
A. L. Sifton (L)	1910 — 1917
Charles Stewart (L)	1917 — 1921
Herbert Greenfield (UFA)	1921 — 1925
John Brownlee (UFA)	1925 — 1934
R. G. Reid (UFA)	1934 — 1935
William Aberhart (SC)	1935 — 1943
E. C. Manning (SC)	1943 — 1968
H. E. Strom (SC)	1968 — 1971
Peter Lougheed (PC)	1971 —

and when needed travel to outlying points 'on circuit.'

Justices of the Queen's Bench are appointed by Ottawa. Some are designed to serve in the Queen's Bench appeals court, hearing appeals from both the Queen's Bench and the Provincial Court. The appeals court sits in Edmonton or Calgary, as convenient.

The trial courts of the Queen's Bench hear both civil and criminal cases, usually the more severe ones. Certainly the great majority of cases in both categories are heard by the Provincial Court, with its judges appointed by the province.

The Provincial Court hears civil cases of lesser seriousness, particularly 'small claims' (involving amounts of up to $1000) and domestic disputes (heard in the family court). The Provincial Court has extensive jurisdiction in crim-

inal cases, but in certain situations must commit offenders for trial by the Queen's Bench. In addition it has absolute jurisdiction in 'quasi-criminal' cases, those involving offences against provincial statutes and municipal by-laws.

The handsome courts building in Edmonton is the headquarters of Alberta's judiciary.

DECISION MAKING

The provincial election of 1979 provided Peter Lougheed's Progressive Conservatives with 74 seats in the legislature and the combined opposition parties with a total of five. That left little scope for the adversary system on which legislative procedure is supposed to be based.

Under the adversary system, the ministers who comprise the cabinet are answerable to the legislature for the activities of their departments. Members of the opposition question and criticize these activities, and also the policies on which they are based. So small an opposition cannot hope to do an adequate job.

With the opposition severely limited, the real decision-making takes place behind the scenes. Some issues are clear cut, but others involve conflicts of in-

Alberta's legislature in session. Members address the speaker, who sits at the head of the chamber. The government sits to the speaker's right, and the opposition to his left.

Local Authorities

The provincial government has the higher profile, but municipalities are closer to the people. Municipalities draw their power from the province, and are responsible for providing ser-

vices like police and fire protection, garbage and sewage disposal, water, and road maintenance including snow removal.

Some of the municipalities are urban, some rural. Urban municipalities include cities, towns, 'new towns' (with special borrowing powers), villages, and 'summer villages' (resort areas). Each assesses and collects its own taxes and puts them to use on behalf of the community.

Rural authorities include municipal districts (averaging 30 townships) and rural counties (averaging 40 townships). The difference between them is that in municipal districts school boards are elected independently, whereas in rural counties the council and school board are one and the same.

'Improvement districts' are the outlying areas of Alberta which do not have their own councillors and are directly administered by the Department of Municipal Affairs. One curiosity among the municipalities is the City of Lloydminster, which spans the Saskatchewan boundary and is chartered by both provinces. It is administered by a single elected council under the laws of Saskatchewan.

Edmonton's city hall, the home of one of Alberta's most powerful municipal governments.

terest between different departments. These conflicts have to be resolved before new legislation can be introduced, in the last resort through majority decision in the cabinet.

Five steps are involved before new legislation is brought before the house. First, a proposal is outlined by a department, perhaps on the suggestion of its minister. Second, the proposal is fleshed out and submitted to other departments for their reactions.

Next, the proposal is forwarded to one of five cabinet committees, each dealing with a specific field. One is concerned with social issues, another with the economy, and the others with energy matters, metropolitan affairs, and rural affairs. All ministers are entitled to sit on these committees, but most attend only the meetings that affect their departments.

The committees help to lighten the workload of the cabinet as a whole. Proposals may be referred back to the department concerned for fresh input, or passed on to the finance priorities and co-ordination committee, the fourth stage in the process. This is the body that considers the budgetary implications of the proposal.

The finance committee consists of senior ministers including the premier and is the equivalent of the Treasury Board in other provinces. Besides evaluating new proposals it makes an annual review of programs already in effect, and each year prepares the budget that is presented to the legislature in the spring.

New proposals sanctioned by the finance priorities and co-ordination committee go forward to the full cabinet. Most are adopted without demur, but there is still a chance that a contentious proposal will be rejected. Even so, the idea of the system is to minimize conflicts at cabinet level and so save on ministerial time.

Once passed by the cabinet, the proposal is framed as a bill for introduction to the legislature. There it will be debated, and assuming it is passed, it will go to the lieutenant-governor as representative of the Crown. Only with his signature will the bill become law, but it has been a long time since an Albertan lieutenant-governor refused his assent.

Alberta and Ottawa

Since the early days, Albertans have been deeply suspicious of Eastern Canada. They used to resent being dominated by a federal government in which they had little say, and by financial institutions chiefly concerned with the well-being of the central provinces.

Today Alberta is in a much stronger position, thanks to its petroleum revenues. Even so, the federal government still exerts considerable influence over matters that deeply affect Alberta's prosperity, particularly energy policy and transportation. In Ottawa, Alberta's interests must be balanced against those of Canada as a whole.

Since the 1920s, Albertans have tended to vote anti-Liberal, an expression of their distaste for Eastern Canada. Farmer ('Progressive') candidates were returned to Ottawa as early as 1921, and from the 1930s they were joined by Social Crediters and socialists of the Co-operative Commonwealth Federation.

By World War II the Progressives were in disarray, and in 1942 they were absorbed by the Conservatives

In 1977 Alberta's Indians remembered the signing of Treaty No. 7 a century earlier, and re-enacted the event in the presence of Prince Charles.

who promptly renamed themselves. In the election of 1957, the Progressive Conservatives soundly trounced the Liberals, chiefly through the personality of John Diefenbaker, who was regarded more warmly in Alberta than in his native Saskatchewan.

Since then, Alberta's conservatism has never been in doubt. The Diefenbaker years ended in 1966, but ten years later an Albertan was elected leader of the federal Conservatives. In 1979 Joe Clark of High River became Canada's prime minister, the only Albertan to attain the office apart from R. B. Bennett of Calgary who was born in New Brunswick.

One group of Albertans is dependent on Ottawa to the exclusion of the provincial government. Status Indians live on the reserves agreed on by their forefathers and are administered by the federal Department of Indian Affairs and Northern Development. The Bloods' reserve, close to Cardston, is the largest in Canada.

REVENUES

Albertans pay the lowest taxes in Canada. Personal income tax is lower than elsewhere, gasoline tax has been abolished, and the government has never imposed a sales tax. Instead, the province depends on royalties paid by companies that exploit its non-renewable resources.

Oil is the most valuable of these resources, but natural gas, coal, and others also contribute. The resources belong to the people of Alberta, and the government collects both royalties and taxes on their behalf. In all, sales of non-renewable resources provide more than 60 per cent of the government's total revenues.

Before 1976, all revenues became part of the general budgetary fund used to pay for the government's services. Following the energy crisis of the early 1970s, however, revenues increased dramatically. The government was receiving far more money than it was prepared to spend, and a large surplus was created.

Wondering how to dispose of the surplus, the government considered a number of alternatives. One was to abolish personal taxes altogether, but that would have set off an immediate invasion of outsiders. Another was to distribute funds to the people, just as Aberhart's Social Crediters had wanted to do with their social dividends.

A third possibility was to invest the surplus, and this was the most attractive. It stood to reason that non-renewable resources would one day be exhausted, and it seemed certain that it would be increasingly costly to exploit them. Profits would be lower, and revenues would decline.

To provide for Alberta's future, the government decided to create the Alberta Heritage Savings Trust Fund. Thirty per cent of all revenues from the sale of non-renewable resources would be transferred to the fund, which would aim to improve the quality of life in Alberta and make investments for the future.

Kananaskis provincial park in the Rockies, one of the projects made possible by the Alberta Heritage Savings Trust Fund.

Alberta is using the proceeds of non-renewable resources to enhance renewable resources. One project is the upgrading of irrigation schemes in the south of the province, extending the network of ditches that carries water to the farmlands.

Considerable sums from the Heritage Savings Trust Fund have been used to expand Alberta's health care facilities, among them the Health Sciences Centre in Edmonton.

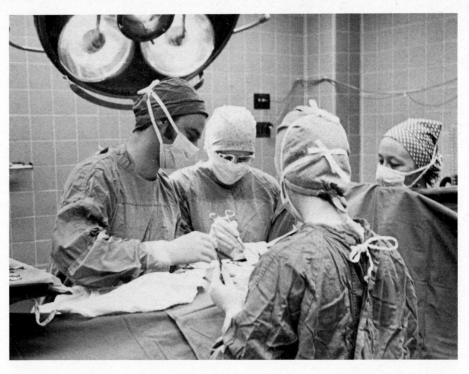

The fund came into being in 1976, and its assets were soon worth several billions of dollars. According to the legislation that created it, up to 20 per cent of what it contained could be invested in capital projects with long-term economic or social benefits for the people of Alberta.

Appropriately, some of the proceeds of non-renewable resources are being used to enhance renewable resources. In the south, the headwaters of irrigation districts are being upgraded and extended. For the north, a new reforestation nursery has been opened at Pine Ridge north-east of Edmonton.

Heritage funds have been used to develop a huge new mountain park, Kananaskis south of Banff, as well as Fish Creek park in Calgary and Capital City park in Edmonton. New books about Alberta, upgraded health care facilities, improved transportation links, and extensive research programs have also been provided.

A second division of the fund is designed to benefit other parts of Canada. Up to 15 per cent of the total can be loaned to the government of Canada or to other provincial governments, or loaned to other institutions on their guarantee. The first governments to be granted loans were those of Newfoundland, New Brunswick, and Manitoba.

The third and largest division of the fund is earmarked for investments that will yield a profit. The investments can be made in Canada or outside, but the aim is to strengthen and diversify Alberta's economy and gain the best possible return. Dividends are added to the fund and are then available for reinvestment.

Together, the three investment divisions utilize most of the money in the fund, but there is always some left over. This money can be used for short-term investments of many types at the discretion of the provincial treasurer. The aim is to make the money work.

In some respects, the Heritage Fund is not really necessary. Its many projects could be funded from the ordinary budgetary surplus. On the other hand, the fund is valuable in reminding Albertans that resource revenues are being put to good use. Besides, the investment program is self-perpetuating.

The fund is controlled by a special investment committee, in fact the cabinet, which is answerable to the legislature. It is administered by the Alberta Treasury, just like the general budgetary fund. With its huge assets, the fund is steadily expanding, and it provides an impressive reserve against a rainy day.

Mining operations have left unfortunate eyesores in the Rockies, but in several instances the Alberta Heritage Savings Trust Fund has made it possible to landscape the terrain, perhaps turning the abandoned open pit into a lake.

SCHOOLS AND COLLEGES

When William Aberhart led his Social Crediters to power in 1935, he became minister of education as well as premier. His cabinet included several other former schoolteachers, and it was plain that the new government would place great importance on educational reform.

At the time, Alberta's school system was a hodgepodge of more than 1500 autonomous school districts. Many were Protestant, some Roman Catholic, and most were responsible for a one-room school staffed by a single teacher. High schools were few and far between, and the subjects taught were academic and narrowly defined.

The Social Crediters wanted to reorganize the system and relax the curriculum. They were influenced by new approaches to education being pioneered in the United States, in particular the 'enterprise' teaching method that encouraged students to learn by doing.

Enterprise teaching is now familiar throughout Canada, but it was first introduced in Alberta. So was the notion of a core curriculum, with the barriers between subjects broken down and bridges created between them. Alberta was the first province to abandon separate history and geography courses in favour of social studies.

In reorganizing the school system, the Social Crediters first encouraged the rural school districts to federate as school divisions. Today, there are 30 such divisions, each including between 70 and 80 districts. The districts still elect trustees to advise on local matters, but the divisional boards are responsible for engaging teachers, building schools, and transporting students.

From 1950, the federated divisions were incorporated with municipal school districts on a county basis. Before that happened, the Social Crediters refined the system by splitting it three ways. Grades 1 to 6 were designated 'elementary,' Grades 7 to 9 were 'junior high,' and Grades 10 to 12 were 'high school' — still the arrangement today.

Another special contribution of the Social Crediters was to upgrade the status of the teaching profession. Until World War II, teachers were trained in 'normal schools' and were notoriously underpaid. From 1945 the Social Crediters aimed to pay them more and train them longer. The normal schools were merged as a faculty of education at the University of Alberta.

Today, the province is served by two distinct school systems — public schools for the religious majority (whether Protestant or Roman Catholic), and separate schools for the minority. Both public and separate school boards provide French-medium schools where required, and also German- or Ukrainian-medium instruction if there is a demand.

Student electricians at a college in Fort McMurray. There are similar colleges in all the major centres of Alberta, each offering courses in technical and vocational subjects.

From high school, many students proceed to higher education. There are four universities in Alberta, as well as eight community colleges offering courses that lead on to university. These colleges are located in Calgary (Mount Royal), Edmonton (Grant MacEwan), Lethbridge, Medicine Hat, Red Deer, Grande Prairie, Vermilion, Lloydminster, and Fort McMurray.

Several of the colleges offer technical training, and there are three agricultural colleges and two technical institutes — the Southern Alberta Institute of Technology (SAIT) in Calgary, opened in 1916, and the Northern Alberta Institute of Technology (NAIT) opened in Edmonton in the 1960s.

A high school class in St. Paul, a town with a strong francophone heritage.

Universities

There are four universities in Alberta, three of them organized on residential lines and the fourth radically different. The senior of the four is the University of Alberta in Edmonton, founded in 1908 with an initial enrolment of 45 students.

From that modest beginning, the university quickly expanded. In 1911 it moved to its present campus. By the end of the first decade there were four faculties — Arts and Science, Law, Applied Science (including medicine), and Agriculture. In the 1920s four more were added, and today there are 14.

Gradually the university's influence spread beyond Edmonton. An extension department was formed 'to bring the university to the people of Alberta.' A summer offshoot, the Banff School of Fine Arts, was opened in 1933. From 1945, branches of faculties were opened in Calgary, which had no university of its own.

Today, the University of Alberta is one of Western Canada's biggest, with nearly 19 000 full-time students enrolled. That compares with nearly 11 000 at the University of Calgary, which became independent of the University of Alberta in 1965. Calgary's university

The campus of the University of Calgary, which became independent of the University of Alberta in 1965.

has 12 faculties, including Medicine, Law, Business, and Education.

Both Edmonton and Calgary are becoming important as research centres, and land has been reserved near the universities to hold research complexes. Alberta's third university is in Lethbridge, opened in 1967 and offering a number of undergraduate programs. Lethbridge's campus is sited high in a coulee above the Oldman river.

Athabasca university in Edmonton is the exception. It was originally proposed by Alberta's Social Crediters in 1970 to ease congestion at the other universities, but suddenly enrolment slackened. In 1972 the new Progressive Conservative government decided that the institution should cater to students working at home.

Today, Athabasca university has offices in Edmonton, but there are no tuition facilities. Instead, each student receives texts and tapes relating to a course, and eventually writes examinations on the material. Athabasca's courses are especially designed to cross the barriers that separate subjects in more formal educational systems.

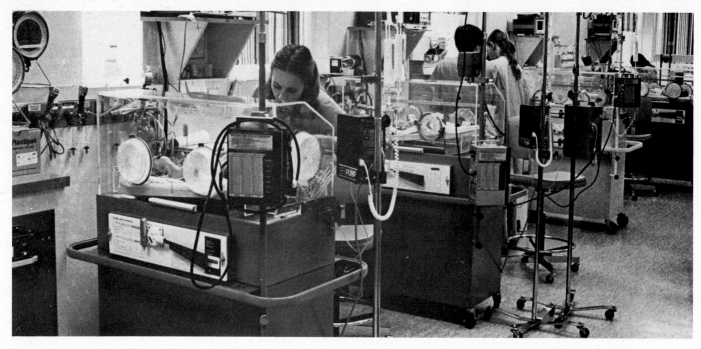

THE HOSPITALS

One way in which the Alberta Heritage Savings Trust Fund is being put to work is in providing new hospitals. In Calgary, the children's hospital has been enlarged and a cancer centre has been established. In Edmonton, the Health Sciences Centre begun in 1977 is one of the most advanced in North America.

Physiotherapists help patients recovering from surgery to regain the use of their limbs and prepare for the world outside.

Heritage funds have been used to build hospitals, but not to operate them. As in all Alberta's hospitals, operating costs are shared by three authorities — the owner (often the local municipality), the province, and the federal government. Much of the province's share is covered by premiums paid into Alberta's Health Care Insurance Plan.

Health services in Alberta fall into four broad categories, apart from the attentions of general practitioners and specialists whose services are usually covered by the provincial health plan. Included in the categories are general

Premature babies are nursed in incubators at Edmonton's Health Sciences Centre, one of the most advanced health complexes in North America.

hospitals, auxiliary hospitals, nursing homes, and community health services.

The general hospitals range from huge institutions like the Health Sciences Centre and Calgary General (with nearly 1000 beds) to the simple facilities found in smaller communities that specialize in primary care. Rural hospitals usually refer more serious cases to the major centres of the two big cities.

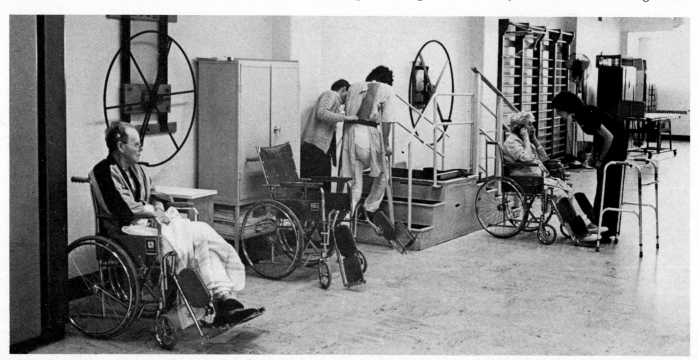

Nursing staff of an intensive care unit treat a patient suffering from heart disease.

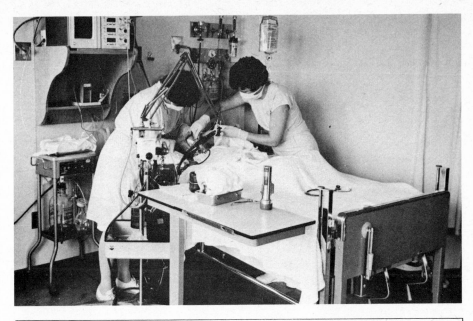

Improved transport links have reduced the importance of rural hospitals. In the past, nearly all of them had surgical programs and could offer acute care (that is, care involving specialized treatment). Now, many concentrate on emergencies and outpatients, and their beds are occupied by patients who need extended care or supervised nursing.

Alberta's population has increased more rapidly than the number of hospital beds available, and the large hospitals often have waiting lists of patients requiring treatment. Increasingly, patients are spending a minimum period in acute care facilities, and are then transferred to an auxiliary hospital.

Auxiliary hospitals specialize in extended care, whether for the terminally ill, the permanently disabled, the short-term convalescent, or the long-term patient needing rehabilitation. Treatment costs per bed are much lower than in acute care hospitals, and there is less of an accommodation problem.

Even less costly are Alberta's nursing homes. The homes are for people who have no need of intensive medical care, but do require looking after because of age or mental or physical problems. Some of the homes are private, some public, and the province subsidizes patients who are Alberta residents.

In all there are some 75 nursing homes in Alberta, compared with about 130 general hospitals and more than 30 auxiliary hospitals. These institutions are supported by a full program of community health services. Edmonton and Calgary have their own public health units, and nearly 30 rural units serve the rest of the province.

The typical community health unit is staffed by a physician, a public health nurse, a dental officer and dental auxiliary, public health inspectors, and perhaps a speech therapist. Service is free and includes everything from pre-natal training to enforcement of provincial regulations covering housing, food, and water.

At the University of Alberta's school of nursing, an instructor shows students how to lift a patient in fragile condition.

Preventive Medicine

Acute care hospitals have become sophisticated and therefore expensive. Trying to keep costs down, Alberta's government is spending less on treating the sick and more on keeping people healthy so that they will not need hospital treatment.

In part, this has involved reducing the funds made available to the acute care hospitals. Rather than expand to accommodate more patients, the hospitals are reserving their beds for those who really need them. Other patients are being treated in auxiliary hospitals where costs are lower, or at home.

Even more important is public education. Albertans are being urged to keep fit through exercise, not to smoke, and not to drink too much. To cut down on injury through motor accidents, they are being urged to wear seatbelts, though paradoxically Alberta's speed limit is unusually high and seatbelt use is not obligatory.

Perhaps most significant, the University of Alberta's medical school has radically revised its approach to treatment. In the past, medical education concentrated on exceptional illness and the appropriate remedies. Today, it focusses on health rather than sickness — the positive rather than the negative. Tomorrow's doctors are being taught that the less they are needed, the better.

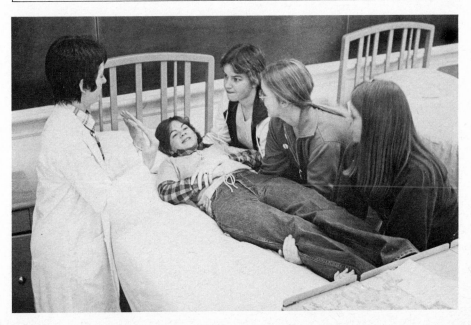

RELIGION

Settlers reaching Alberta from around the world introduced their religious beliefs and kept them alive as part of their heritage. Some are familiar across Canada, some much less common, but the variety encourages a high level of religious tolerance.

Christianity reached the region in the days of the fur trade, and there was keen rivalry between Presbyterian missionaries and their Roman Catholic counterparts. Anglicans and Wesleyans arrived later, ministering to homesteaders and establishing churches that survive to the present.

The wave of immigration from Eastern Europe introduced new Christian denominations like the Ukrainian Catholic and Ukrainian Orthodox churches. In some areas their onion-domed places of worship have become as familiar as prairie grain elevators, and their celebrations of Christmas and Easter are especially colourful.

Ukrainian churches, both Catholic and Orthodox, are to be seen in the cities and in areas of Ukrainian settlement.

Mormons of the Church of Jesus Christ of Latter Day Saints entered Alberta in the 1880s, sent from their home state of Utah to create new colonies. The first party founded the town now named Cardston in honour of their leader, Charles Ora Card.

Ora Card's homestead has been preserved, and Cardston is the site of the only Mormon temple in Canada. Non-Mormons are forbidden access to the temple, but guides are on hand to explain Mormon beliefs and the lifestyle of the faithful.

Hutterites, members of a conservative Christian sect permitted to settle in Canada after World War I, are even more exclusive than the Mormons. Living according to precepts laid down centuries ago, Hutterite colonists pledge themselves to share their possessions and to obey leaders who are elected democratically.

A typical Hutterite colony consists of up to a dozen families, in total perhaps 100 people including children. The colonists eat together, work together, and worship together, and they take pride in their self-sufficiency since they make their own clothes and build their own houses. At the same time they are among Alberta's most efficient farmers.

The Hutterites follow ideals laid down by Jacob Hutter, an Anabaptist of of the fifteenth century, just as Lutherans remain loyal to his contemporary, Martin Luther. The Lutheran church is well represented throughout Alberta, and Lutheran missionaries are active in the north.

The Dutch Reformed church, branches of the Mennonite faith, and many other Christian denominations are to be found in Alberta. Many of them are represented on Edmonton's 96th Street, reputed to hold a greater variety of places of worship than any other street in North America.

Besides its Christians, Edmonton also possesses a significant community of Ismaili Moslems, the followers of the Aga Khan. A mosque built in Edmonton

Hutterites entered Alberta from the United States after World War I and have founded a number of colonies in which they live simply and share all their possessions.

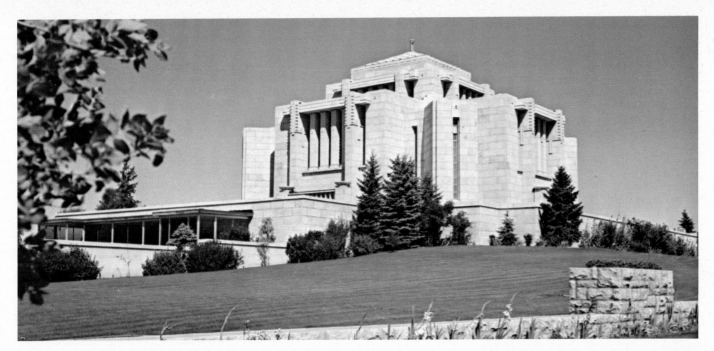

in the 1940s is the oldest in Canada, and Moslems arriving more recently have built mosques in unexpected locations including Lac La Biche.

Both Calgary and Edmonton have significant Jewish communities, and the Lethbridge area holds a number of Buddhists. The Buddhists are of Japanese descent, many of them transplanted from the coast of British Columbia during World War II because they were suspected of collaborating with the enemy.

Buddhist influence is strong in Lethbridge's Japanese Friendship Garden, a tranquil environment recalling

The Mormon Temple in Cardston, the only one in Canada. Mormons were among Alberta's earliest settlers.

the elements of a Buddhist monastery. The garden is a special pride of all the Japanese in Alberta, even though many of them are practising Christians.

The Sundance

Christian missionaries trying to convert the Blackfoot took violent exception to an elaborate religious ceremony known as the sundance. Partly public and partly secret, the dance took place on holy ground during the course of several days.

The procedure followed in the sundance varied from tribe to tribe, but in all cases the aim was to achieve purity in the face of the sun, the giver of life. Women played the key roles in the secret parts of the ceremony, but it was the men who built the elaborate brushwood lodge in which it took place.

The missionaries were not outraged by the dance itself, but by the demonstrations of self-torture that often accompanied it. Young warriors attached lines to wooden skewers inserted in the loose skin of their chests. Then they strained backwards to pull the skewers through the skin, and so prove their manhood.

In time, the sundance was banned by the government, but some Indians continued to celebrate it. In recent years there has been a strong resurgence of interest in the dance, which was traditionally the most important of all Indian ceremonies. In the sundance, today's Indians can remember their ancestors and keep their culture alive.

The skeleton of a sundance lodge, not far from the Rockies. In spite of missionaries' efforts to curb the ceremony, Indians still regard it as an essential part of their heritage.

ARTS AND LETTERS

Alberta was the last of Canada's provinces to be settled, but it has already produced a number of artists and writers whose work has made its mark far from home. Some were born in Alberta, some arrived from elsewhere, and some left for elsewhere.

Of the artists, two now live in British Columbia. Max Bates was born in Calgary and pioneered expressionism in Western Canada. H. G. Glyde arrived in Alberta from Britain and, like Bates, proved a keen observer of the human

Students at the Alberta College of Art in Calgary, one of Canada's leading art schools. Painters and sculptors are better supported in Calgary than anywhere else in the country.

Alberta Culture

In Calgary, proud Hungarians introduce their daughters at a debutantes' ball. In Lethbridge, kimonoed Japanese study the intricacies of the tea ceremony. In Fort McMurray, Irish Albertans gather to celebrate St. Patrick's Day. In Vegreville, Ukrainians decorate eggs and exchange them to celebrate Easter.

These are just a few of scores of deep-rooted traditions introduced by Alberta's pioneers. From Scandinavian weddings to East Indian New Year, celebrations from other parts of the world are becoming as familiar as spring planting and the fall round-up, and ethnic communities are inviting their neighbours to join in.

The largest ethnic grouping is of British origin, but it includes many families that lived in the United States before settling in Alberta. The second largest group is of German origin. The third largest, drawn from the Ukraine, is the closest-knit of all the ethnic communities, celebrating its heritage in song, dance, and many other ways.

Edmonton and Calgary are melting pots of many cultures, but in rural Alberta ethnic communities have tended to identify themselves with particular regions. Ukrainians are found in the parklands and in the Peace river country, Dutch farmers in the irrigated lands south and east of Calgary.

There are many French-speakers in north-central and northern Alberta. In the Lethbridge region there are many Japanese market gardeners, brought to Alberta after being expelled from British Columbia's coastal islands during World War II. Hutterite colonies abound, and Scandinavians have long been prominent in both the north and the south.

Koreans, Lebanese, Czechs, West Indians, Greeks — all these groups add to Alberta's diversity. Alberta helps them by supporting efforts to keep their many languages alive, and by holding an annual Alberta Heritage Day to celebrate their contributions and those of all Alberta's pioneers.

Regalia of the Plains Indians is preserved at Glenbow museum in Calgary, together with reminders of the other peoples who made Alberta what it is.

scene. William Kurelek, who died in 1977, was born in the Vegreville area. He left Alberta at the age of six, but later in life painted his impressions of a prairie boyhood. Roloff Beny of Medicine Hat started his career as a painter, but in the 1950s switched to photography.

Edmonton takes an interest in Alberta's visual arts, but Calgary provides most of the support. Calgary is the home of the Alberta College of Art and has more galleries per capita than any other community in Canada. Private collectors abound, and many corporations are buying the works of Albertan artists as an investment.

Of the better-known writers, most were not born in Alberta. The novelists W. O. Mitchell and Rudy Wiebe arrived from Saskatchewan, and the popular historians James Gray and Grant MacEwan were originally from Manitoba. J. G. MacGregor, Alberta's best-known historian, was brought from Scotland at the age of one.

The novelist Robert Kroetsch was

Calgary is unusually well blessed with museums and art galleries, some public and some private. This is the gallery at the Alberta College of Art.

born on a farm near Red Deer, and the poet Earle Birney, who now lives in B.C., grew up in Calgary. Several younger talents have come to light through the provincial government's Search-for-a-New-Alberta-Novelist competition. The 1975 winner was Pauline Gedge with her *Child of the Morning*, which has since had great success in Canada, the United States, and Britain.

The library of the University of Calgary is collecting the papers of contemporary Canadian writers, and Albertans are well represented. W. O. Mitchell and Rudy Wiebe are among them. The collection also includes the papers of notable outsiders like Hugh MacLennan, Mordecai Richler, Bruce Hutchison, and Andre Langevin.

H. G. Glyde's *Miners at Canmore*, **an oil painting completed in 1950. Canmore is located in the Bow river valley just outside Banff National Park.**

Shumka, one of several outstanding Ukrainian dance troupes based in Alberta. Here, Shumka poses in Edmonton before flying to tour Japan.

The Edmonton Symphony in concert. Symphony and choral music is flourishing both in Edmonton and Calgary, and several smaller communities have their own orchestras.

THE PERFORMERS

Calgary has a commanding lead in the visual arts, but Edmonton's theatre, ballet, symphony, and opera make it the envy of communities across the country. Edmonton has sophisticated facilities that Calgary lacks, but Calgary is building a large civic centre that will include a major auditorium.

Theatre is the flagship of the performing arts. Calgary's leading company is Theatre Calgary, a professional group that performs in a converted warehouse. Edmonton's is the Citadel Theatre, which took its name from the old Salvation Army citadel where it was based until 1976.

Today, the Citadel's home is one of the most luxurious theatres in North America, close to the heart of Edmonton. Opened in 1976, the new Citadel is a palace of glass that contains three separate auditoriums. One of them is for major productions, one is for experimental work, and one is a film theatre.

To the envy of other theatres in Canada, the Citadel is 90 per cent subscribed — a measure of its popularity in Edmonton. It could be 100 per cent subscribed, but the theatre deliberately keeps back seats for those not wanting tickets for the whole season, which extends through fall and winter.

Outside the major companies, alternate theatre is strong. In Edmonton there is Theatre 3 (named when the Citadel had only two stages) and Calgary has Alberta Theatre Projects. Both present experimental works. Walterdale Associates in Edmonton and the Pumphouse Theatre in Calgary are semi-professional repertory groups.

Both Edmonton and Calgary have thriving opera companies, as yet only semi-professional. Calgary's is the Southern Alberta Opera Association, which performs in the Jubilee Auditorium. There is a Jubilee Auditorium in Edmonton too, like Calgary's owned by the province, and it is the home of Edmonton Opera Association.

The two auditoriums are also used for performances of the cities' professional symphony orchestras, the Edmonton Symphony and the Calgary Philharmonic. Both orchestras are well known across Canada, and in the 1970s the Edmonton Symphony broke new ground when concerts with artists like Tom Jones and Anne Murray were televised worldwide.

Musical instruction is especially strong in Calgary, and the city has produced a number of smaller musical groups fast making names for themselves. Among them are the Alberta Chamber Players, a string orchestra, and One Third Ninth, a piano trio. Edmonton's response is the Plumbers' Union, a quartet of recorder players.

In the world of dance, the Alberta Ballet is Canada's only professional ballet company west of Winnipeg. Based in Edmonton, the company presents both classical and modern material. The Alberta Contemporary Dance Theatre is another Edmonton company becoming known across Canada.

Ukrainian dance ensembles like Cheremosh, Shumka, and Dnipro are among the liveliest amateur groups in Alberta. All three are in Edmonton. Of the individual performers based in the province, the most successful has been the harpist Carol McLaughlin of Calgary, who is in demand all through North America.

Choirs, amateur theatre groups, and many other elements contribute to the cultural mosaics of Alberta's major centres. The same spirit is present in many of the other communities too. At least four of them have community orchestras, and more than 100 have formed arts organizations that invite touring performers to their region.

To contact these performers, representatives from the arts organizations converge on Edmonton for the annual Alberta Showcase. Musicians, dancers, singers, and performing groups from all over the province go through their paces, hoping for bookings. The exposure helps the performers, and Alberta Showcase helps the arts organizations to sample the best of what is available.

Behind the scenes at the Banff festival, a summer attraction that combines theatre, music, and all the performing arts.

SPORT AND RECREATION

One of Alberta's paradoxes is that it is poised on two distinct frontiers. One is the western frontier and the other is the north, and each has special traditions that are well represented in the Albertan lifestyle.

On the simplest analogy, the western frontier encourages aggressive in-

Young girls enjoy a game of waterpolo in a Calgary swimming pool.

stincts while the north demands defence. Westerners' driving influence has been the hope of profit, while northerners have been chiefly concerned with survival. The west suggests teamwork, the north, independence and self-reliance.

Both these approaches are represented in Alberta's sports world. Team sports like football, hockey, curling, and basketball are popular in most parts of the province, but so are sports for individuals like fishing, skiing, and horseback riding.

The sport that excites most interest in Alberta is football, played at least since the 1890s. The province has two professional franchises in the Canadian Football League, the Calgary Stampeders and the Edmonton Eskimos, and both have fared well in Grey Cup competition.

Calgarians in particular have turned the Grey Cup final into a celebration wherever it is played. Their team won the cup in 1948 and again in 1971. The Edmonton Eskimos won in three successive years between 1954 and 1956 and won again in 1975 and 1978.

Another professional franchise, the Edmonton Oilers, was originally part of the World Hockey Association and was accepted into the National Hockey League in 1979. The Edmonton Drillers play in the North American Soccer

In Alberta curling is nearly as popular as hockey, and Albertan rinks are among the world's best.

League. None of these teams has come close to matching the record of an amateur squad that made Edmonton famous between the wars — the Grads, women basketball players who were the most successful sports team that Canada has produced.

Between 1915 and 1940 the Edmonton Grads played 522 games and won 502 of them. They defeated all comers in exhibition matches at the Olympic games of 1924, 1928, 1932, and 1936. Once they had a winning streak of 147 games, and another time it was 78. Against American opponents they won 138 games out of 152.

Two generations of Edmonton girls played for the Grads. Their success came from the contributions of the man who founded and coached them, John Percy Page. In 1940 Page disbanded the team because the Canadian air force was taking over the Edmonton arena. By that time there was no team left to challenge them.

If the Grads were still playing today, they would not have to disband through lack of facilities. All over the province sports and recreational facilities have been improved, and young Albertans are taking advantage of them. Even tiny

Commonwealth Games

In the summer of 1978 Edmonton played host to the Commonwealth Games. Held every four years, the event is known as the 'friendly games,' because it is designed to be 'merrier and less stern' than international competitions where pressure is intense.

Edmonton prepared for the games by building new facilities including a multi-purpose stadium, a covered aquatic centre, and a velodrome. All were ready with time to spare, and a large corps of volunteers was recruited to help run the games cheaply and efficiently.

More than 40 Commonwealth countries sent competitors to the games. They were to compete in ten sports — track and field athletics, badminton, boxing, cycling, gymnastics, lawn bowling, shooting, swimming and diving, weightlifting, and wrestling. Lacrosse was added to the roster as a demonstration sport.

The Canadian team as a whole fared exceptionally well in the games and won more medals than any other team. Many of the medals went to Albertans, among them Graham Smith of Edmonton who won six gold medals in the swimming. Other Albertans won

in track and field, shooting, boxing, and weightlifting.

The games lasted ten days and proved an unqualified success. A cultural festival accompanying the games threatened to eclipse the sporting events, particularly as eight Commonwealth nations sent their national dance troupes. Edmonton's legacy was

The Commonwealth Stadium in Edmonton, built for the Commonwealth Games of 1978. It is now the permanent home of the Edmonton Eskimos of the Canadian Football League.

well-justified pride that the city could organize such a lavish spectacle, and impressive facilities that would be invaluable for decades to come.

communities have hockey and curling arenas, and swimming pools for the summer.

In many cases these communities are assisted by the provincial government, which pays for the facilities and encourages people to use them. Current thinking is that recreation meets an essential social need, for if increased leisure time is used unwisely, it can be a danger as well as a boon.

One outstanding recreational facility has been made possible through private enterprise. Spruce Meadows, the equine sports centre outside Calgary, is regarded as the finest of its type in Canada. It attracts international competition in show jumping, dressage, and other equestrian events.

There is fine fishing in many of Alberta's rivers and lakes, as here on the North Saskatchewan river. The fish to be caught include pike, perch, walleye, and six varieties of trout.

RODEO

Alberta's favourite spectator sport is in a class by itself. Once the diversion of high-spirited cowboys home from the range, rodeo has become a sophisticated industry employing many of Canada's most courageous athletes.

Canada's first rodeo took place in Calgary in 1893, an idea introduced from the United States. There, rodeo had been imported by Mexican cowboys employed in Texas and New Mexico.

Today, there are some 600 professional rodeos organized in North America each year, nearly 50 of them in Alberta.

Beginning in Lethbridge in March, Canadian rodeo competitors travel from location to location until October. The most successful take part in the Canadian rodeo finals in November, held in Edmonton. Albertans take part in events at home and in other provinces, and not a few are in the front rank of rodeo stars in the United States.

The competitors fall into three chief categories — riders, ropers, and wrestlers. Riders tend to be small and agile, like jockeys. Ropers and wrestlers have to be bigger and stronger. Some competitors learn their skills in a work situation like the cowboys of old, but an increasing number start with little or no experience and begin from scratch in a rodeo school.

Rodeo riders normally specialize in one of three events, all tests of their reflexes and sense of balance. One is bareback bronc riding, a wild spurring

Calgary Stampede

In 1912 a Wyoming cowboy, Guy Weadick, persuaded four Calgarian businessmen to sponsor 'the greatest frontier day celebration ever.' So was born the world-famous Calgary Stampede, one of the four biggest rodeos of North America.

Weadick's first rodeo was a success in every way except financially. Not until 1919 were the sponsors ready to back a second try, but that time they made a profit. Since 1923 the stampede has been an annual event, held in conjunction with the Calgary Exhibition, a major agricultural show

first held in 1885.

To celebrate his brainchild's new prestige, Weadick devised the event that has been a Calgary specialty ever since — the chuckwagon race. Rules have changed since the early days, but the basic components of a chuckwagon team are still a regulation round-up wagon hauled by four horses and attended by four outriders.

Today, each chuckwagon race involves four outfits. The outriders start dismounted, and load stoves, tent poles, and canvas into their wagons. Then the drivers race their teams around barrels in a figure-of-eight, and start the one-kilometre dash to the

finish with the outriders in hot pursuit.

Other attractions at Calgary's stampede include wild cow milking contests, wild horse racing, and Indian buffalo riding. All the classic rodeo competitions are featured, and to start the festival there is a major street parade, with bands, floats, richly costumed Indians, and the best-dressed cowboys and cowgirls in Canada.

In the steer wrestling event, a 'hazer' keeps the steer running straight while the 'bulldogger' leaps from his saddle and catches the steer by the horns. He aims to wrestle it to the ground with all four of the steer's legs extended on the same side.

Bull-riding is rodeo's most dangerous event. The rider holds on to a rope pulled tight around the animal's girth.

event in which the rider has no saddle, rein, or stirrups. Instead, he holds on to a leather rigging with one hand, keeping the other one free of the horse and rolling blunted spurs on its neck to score points.

A bareback rider must last eight seconds without being bucked off. A saddle bronc ride lasts eight or ten seconds, depending on the rodeo. In this event, saddles are standardized and the rider has stirrups and a single rein. Rather than push his feet forwards like a bareback competitor, the saddle rider spurs 'fore and aft.'

The third riding competition is the most dangerous. For eight seconds, competitors ride a bull, holding on to a rope pulled tight around the animal's girth. When the rider dismounts or is bucked off, a gaudily dressed 'clown' intervenes on foot to distract the bull until the rider has escaped to safety.

In each of these riding events, cowboys depend heavily on the quality of the animals they are riding. The more a horse bucks, the more points the rider accumulates. In many cases the animals are bred especially for rodeo work and are as highly regarded as the cowboys. Riders draw lots for them on the day of the competition.

Mounts play a major part in the other rodeo competitions. In calf-roping, the horse stops short as soon as the roper's lariat is around the calf's neck. As the roper dismounts to run forward, the horse rears back to keep the rope tight. The roper upends the calf, then uses a two-metre 'piggin' string' to wrap three of its legs and tie them in a half-hitch.

In 'bulldogging' or steer wrestling, a 'hazer' rides alongside a running steer to keep it heading straight. The 'dogger' rides up on the other side and leaps from his saddle to take the steer by the horns. Using his body weight and scientific leverage, he wrestles the steer off its feet until it is flat with all four legs extended on the same side.

The five classic rodeo competitions are offset by a lively event designed for cowgirls rather than cowboys. One at a time, the girls race around three barrels set about 30 m apart in a triangle. They must circle each barrel completely without knocking it over, and as in the roping and wrestling events, the fastest time wins.

Chuckwagon racing, the highlight of the Calgary Stampede, was devised by Guy Weadick in 1923. In each race, four outfits round barrels and race one kilometre to the finish.

MOUNTAIN PARKS

Construction workers building the CPR in 1883 discovered hot sulphur springs in the heart of the Rockies. The springs were in a glorious setting, and they soon became a tourist attraction. Two of the workers camped near by and began charging admission.

The workers soon became a major embarrassment to the CPR, and there was an angry dispute over ownership. The government of Canada became in-

volved, and on the CPR's suggestion it created a 'national reserve' around the springs, protecting them 'from sale, or settlement, or squatting.' At first the reserve covered 10 km², but it was soon enlarged.

A small resort developed near the springs, which was named 'Banff' after the boyhood home of Lord Strathcona of the CPR. In 1892 a second 'national reserve' was created around Lake Louise, with similar results. Those were the beginnings of Banff National Park,

Spectacular skiing on the slops of Mount Norquay, overlooking the town of Banff. Beyond the town is the famous profile of Mount Rundle.

which has since been enlarged to cover some 6640 km².

Since the early days, the park's spectacular scenery has attracted visitors from all over the world and in all seasons. Many of them bathe in the hot springs that were the original draw, but for others the highlights are gondola rides to the tops of mountains, raft trips

Plains and Foothills

Before 1930 Alberta's Crown lands and natural resources were controlled by the government of Canada. Alberta could create no parks of its own, but the Dominion government set aside two more national parks in addition to the three in the mountains — Elk Island and Wood Buffalo.

Control of Crown lands was transferred in 1930, and Alberta soon passed legislation to establish provincial parks. The first, Aspen Beach near Red

Deer, came into existence in 1932. So did Saskatoon Island near Grande Prairie, Gooseberry Lake in the east, and Park Lake near Lethbridge.

The early provincial parks were small and close to settlements. They were created through local initiative and run by citizens' committees. That was the pattern until the 1950s, by which time transport was better and the provincial parks were attracting outsiders.

Between 1945 and 1965 nearly 30 new provincial parks were brought into being. Many were intended to preserve special natural features. That

was the case with the Cypress Hills provincial park set up in 1945, the second largest in Alberta, and the Sir Winston Churchill park on Lac La Biche, which was originally a bird sanctuary.

Today there are more than 50 provincial parks in Alberta, covering terrain from the badlands to the foothills. Two are especially interesting. Writing-on-Stone park in the badlands of the south preserves 58 prehistoric rock art sites, the largest concentration in Canada. Dinosaur park near Brooks holds reptile remains of world significance.

Moraine Lake south of Lake Louise, beautiful in all seasons and one of the attractions that makes Canada's Rockies world famous.

down the Bow river, or any of 101 recreational ideas that Banff business entrepreneurs have devised.

Mount Rundle overlooking Banff is the most-photographed mountain in Canada. Lake Louise must be the most-photographed lake. Two great hotels, the Banff Springs and the Chateau Lake Louise, look like Scottish castles and are world famous in their own right. To many, the comet-shaped Peyto Lake is the most beautiful feature of all.

Banff's mountain park was a success from the beginning, and Canada's government soon moved to establish more 'national reserves.' One was in Alberta's south-west corner, the beautiful Waterton Lakes National Park established in 1895. It was created on the urging of local residents, notably George 'Kootenai' Brown.

Kootenai Brown became Waterton Lakes' first park warden, and he now lies buried there. The lakes are named after an English naturalist of the eighteenth century, Charles Waterton. The park covers only 600 km², but is famous for 'a maximum of scenery in a minimum of space.' Rolling prairies give way to mountains in the course of a few kilometres.

Jasper National Park, the third great mountain reserve in Alberta, was created in 1907. It was originally an immense expanse of nearly 14 000 km², but has since been pruned to about 11 000 km². There was practically no development of the area until 1915, when a few pioneer tourists were accommodated in tents.

Since then, the townsite of Jasper has developed as a rival to Banff. Pyramid Mountain and Mount Edith Cavell, the Athabasca Falls, and Miette hot springs are all close by. So is the world-famous Maligne Lake with its Spirit Island, reached in the course of a two-hour boat trip through some of the Rockies' most beautiful scenery.

Another special attraction of Jasper

National Park is the Columbia icefield, accessible by the Icefield Parkway that links Jasper with Banff. The parkway passes close to the toe of the Athabasca glacier flowing from the icefield, and visitors venture up its face in buses equipped with snow tracks.

Many Albertans — particularly Edmontonians — say that Jasper is more natural and less commercial than Banff. Certainly it is not nearly as crowded. The pressure on Banff has been so great

that Alberta has established a huge new provincial park to the south, using money from the Alberta Heritage Savings Trust Fund.

The new park is Kananaskis, originally part of the forest reserve system that covers all of Alberta's mountain areas outside the national parks. The scenery in Kananaskis is as glorious as elsewhere, and it has an extra attraction — its Highwood Pass is the highest drivable pass in Canada.

The hot sulphur springs of Banff are still a tourist attraction, even in the depths of winter. Most bathers simply relax in the water and make no effort to swim.

73

Powder skiing at Sunshine Village, about 20 km from Banff and within one-and-a-half hours' drive of Calgary.

A party of mountaineers sets out on a winter climb in the Rockies. Both winter and summer, many mountaineers make use of the climbing huts provided by the Alpine Club of Canada.

THE OUTDOORS

In winter, Alberta's special pride is the ski season of the Rockies' eastern slopes. Snow usually lasts from mid-November until mid-May, and each weekend there is a mass exodus from the cities as skiers head for the 'Big Five' mountain resorts.

Four of the resorts are within 150 km of Calgary, and three of these are in Banff National Park. The most developed is Lake Louise, the largest ski area in Canada. The Lake Louise slopes cover nearly 45 km² and offer 34 designated runs on four separate mountain faces.

The mountain faces catch the sun at different times of the day, and many skiers follow it from one slope to another. They are served by nine skilifts that can handle up to 7600 skiers per hour. Runs are graded 'easiest,' 'more difficult,' or 'most difficult,' and nobody has managed to ski all of them in a single day.

Sunshine Village, the second largest resort, is 20 km from Banff. There, cars are parked five kilometres from the village, and shuttle buses run skiers back and forth. The ski slopes cover some 500 ha, and the five skilifts carry up to 6500 skiers per hour.

Norquay resort is only five kilometres from Banff and is much smaller than the others. Even so, two of its runs are among the most challenging in North America. Its four skilifts can handle up to 1200 skiers an hour, and the resort has a vertical drop of 800 m. The three Banff resorts offer interchangeable lift tickets.

The fourth resort close to Calgary is Fortress Mountain, close to the new Kananaskis provincial park. Opened in 1974, Fortress Mountain has 21 runs and four skilifts that can carry up to 2600 skiers per hour. Like all five resorts, it has a ski school offering special privileges to beginners.

The four southern resorts cater chiefly to Calgarians and other Canadians. Marmot Basin near Jasper attracts large numbers of Edmontonians, in spite of the relatively long drive. Five skilifts carry up to 1200 skiers per hour, and the 25 runs have a vertical drop of nearly 800 m.

Calgarians enjoy the cosmopolitan

excitement of Banff and its exquisite surroundings. Edmontonians say that Jasper is more intimate and less commercial. Unfortunately both have become crowded, and there is pressure on Parks Canada to permit the creation of new resorts elsewhere in the Rockies.

Not all skiers depend on the resorts. There are slopes within Edmonton's city limits, and at other points throughout the province. Some enthusiasts make their way to the Rockies' icefields during summer and ski down a glacier. Cross-country skiers can exercise wherever they find snow.

Cross-country skiing is an older sport than its downhill counterpart and has recently made great headway in Alberta. Part of the reason is the popularity of skiing-mountaineering in spring and fall, when snow is on the ground and mountaineers must use skis to reach the bottoms of the most challenging climbs.

Most of the skiing-mountaineering takes place under the eye of the Alpine Club of Canada, the country's senior mountaineering organization. Founded in 1906, the club has its headquarters near Canmore and has climbing huts in many parts of the Rockies. Its busiest period is July and August, when most slopes are accessible on foot.

Another sport becoming popular in Alberta is trail-riding — five-day expeditions led by experienced outfitters who guide groups of riders through some of the province's most breathtaking scenery. The outfitters are helped by trail bosses who do the cooking and by wranglers who attend to the packhorses.

A typical trail-riding group includes ten paying riders, probably strangers to each other. Some may be experienced, some may never have ridden before. On the trail, they ride in single file with their horses at a walk. Inevitably there is some saddle soreness on the first day or two, but most riders soon learn how to cope with it.

An alternative way to see the Rockies from horseback is to stay at one of Alberta's guest ranches. Most of the ranches have horses for hire, and most are set in delightful countryside. Besides riding, the ranches offer fishing, hiking, skiing in winter, or simply the chance to unwind and relax.

There is white water canoeing in the high country, but the most absorbing river trips are through the forest wilderness of the north. Like fur traders of old, paddlers brave the Peace and Athabasca, or float down the broad North Saskatchewan towards its distant rendezvous with its sister of the south.

Horseback riding on a guest ranch in the foothills. Many visitors embark on long-distance trail-riding expeditions led by experienced outfitters.

75

Among the shyest of Alberta's animals are the mountain goats of the Rockies, nimble-footed creatures that can take refuge on ledges high above the treeline.

Alberta Game Farm

Long before safari parks came into vogue, an Albertan zoologist created a wildlife haven where he could help endangered species. The result is the Alberta Game Farm, a conservation centre that has earned worldwide respect for its remarkable breeding programs.

The game farm is the brainchild of Dr. Al Oeming and was established in 1957. It is located in rolling parkland about 22 km south-east of Edmonton and helps species drawn from many parts of the world. Some herds have grown so large that they need extensive compounds, while others are housed in smaller spaces where visitors can see them at close quarters.

When Al Oeming established the farm, he was afraid that species from warmer climates would never adapt to Alberta's winters. Instead, there have been few problems. In a generation or two, even tropical species endure cold temperatures as readily as those native to Canada. Visiting zoologists are fascinated to see evolution in progress.

Among the game farm's showpieces is the world's largest captive herd of musk oxen, developed from six calves brought from the Northwest Territories in 1960. Three huge grizzly bears arrived at the farm as cubs, and a rare white-coated Kermode bear is from the Prince Rupert area of coastal British Columbia.

Many other Canadian animals are represented at the farm, but for zoologists its major contribution has been in breeding herds of animals faced with extinction. Deer species from China, rare buck from Africa, and tapirs from Indonesia are examples of the wide range of exotic creatures that have made the Alberta Game Farm world famous.

As fall approaches, migrating waterfowl assemble in the Peace-Athasbasca region before embarking on their long journey south for the winter.

WILDLIFE

Alberta's two least-known national parks came into being as wildlife sanctuaries. Elk Island and Wood Buffalo were created to help the species whose names they carry, but in both cases the most spectacular success has been in preserving the bison of the plains.

Elk Island's story began in 1906, at a time when many of the province's large game animals were threatened with extinction. Five Albertans volunteered to fence ten hectares of the Beaver Hills as an elk sanctuary, and the land was provided by the federal government. It was the first such animal sanctuary in Canada.

In the next year, Canada purchased 716 head of plains buffalo from a herd in Montana. At the time, North America's total population of plains bison numbered no more than a few thousand, and only a handful remained in Canada. The plan was to establish the buffalo on a special fenced reserve at Wainwright.

Because the Wainwright reserve was not ready, 400 of the animals were sent to Elk Island where they remained for two years. Most were then rounded up and sent to Wainwright, but nearly 50 escaped capture. Today their descendants still roam the park, nearly 600 strong, and share it with moose, elk, mule deer, and other species that thrive there.

Land has been added to the original Elk Island sanctuary, and the park now covers 30 ha. Wood Buffalo, in contrast, covers nearly 40 000 km², a wilderness area that straddles the boundary between Alberta and the Northwest Territories. The park was created in 1922 to protect Canada's last remaining herd of wood buffalo.

At the time, the herd contained some 1500 buffalo that were larger and darker than their cousins of the plains. Shortly after the park was created, they were joined by more than 6000 plains buffalo shipped north when the Wain-

Significant herds of bison roam the wilds of Wood Buffalo National Park in northern Alberta. Some of the bison are descended from the herd brought from Montana in 1907, some from the bison herds of the northern forests.

wright reserve was abandoned. Unfortunately the two species have intermingled, and the clear distinction is disappearing.

Besides bison, Wood Buffalo holds important populations of woodland caribou and moose, though barren land caribou migrate north-east of the park's boundaries. Furbearers are abundant as in the days of the Nor'Westers, and each fall the Peace-Athabasca delta is the assembly point of millions of waterfowl preparing to migrate south.

Alberta's varied landforms and vegetation patterns are matched by the variety of its wildlife. Timber wolves and black bears roam the boreal forest, but pronghorn antelopes are confined to the arid grassland of the south-east corner. Lynx are found throughout the north and west, and bobcats favour the southern fringe.

Grizzly bears inhabit remote areas of the Rockies and the Swan Hills. Cougars are found in the mountains and sometimes in southern river valleys. High in the Rockies, shaggy mountain goats perch on narrow ledges, and bighorn sheep graze in high meadows above the treeline.

Several hundred species of birds are to be seen in Alberta. Trumpeter swans have recovered from near extinction, and several score of them nest in western Alberta. Sandhill cranes nest north of the Athabasca river, and whooping

Elk were once common in Alberta, but over-hunting in the nineteenth century brought them close to extinction. The species' plight led to the creation of what is now Elk Island National Park, the oldest sanctuary of its type in Canada.

cranes migrate to Alberta's extreme north and over the boundary into the Northwest Territories.

Lakes, rivers, and streams support abundant fish populations. Coldwater species like trout, mountain whitefish, and arctic grayling flourish in 40 per cent of Alberta's waters, and the remainder support warmwater fish like northern pike, walleye, and goldeye.

Constant erosion sculpts the soft stone of the badlands into hoodoos, the 'tombstones of the dinosaurs.' The erosion has exposed the layers of rock sediment that underlie the whole prairie region.

HOODOO MAGIC

Like Americans across the border, Albertans use special terms for many of the geographic features that surround them. Deep ravines in the prairie are 'coulees,' flat-topped hills rising from the plain are 'buttes,' and 'badlands' are rocky regions left barren through erosion.

The badlands contain many spectacular formations, including the famous 'hoodoos' that seem to grow from the rock like giant toadstools. Capped by hard conglomerate that resists the power of the elements, the hoodoos are sculpted as surrounding rock is worn away. Even they are eventually undermined, and topple over as new hoodoos appear around them.

Some of the hoodoos are tiny, some as tall as a house. In their gaunt setting they look like monuments, and some visitors think of them as the tombstones of the dinosaurs. Certainly the badlands seem full of spirits, for Indians used them to dispose of their dead. Perhaps that is why early travellers called the stone formations 'hoodoos,' fearing they had magic powers.

For geologists, the hoodoos provide fascinating insights into the sediments that form Canada's prairies. In layer after layer, they tell the story of millions of years. Brown layers are the evidence of ancient seabeds, rich in marine fossils. Grey layers were formed when the region was covered by swamps and dinosaurs roamed the land.

There are spectacular hoodoos in the valley of the Bow river east of Banff, but the best examples are in the Red Deer badlands. The most accessible are in the Drumheller region and in the Dinosaur provincial park north-east of Brooks. To minimize the risk of damage to the hoodoos, visitors are discouraged from climbing on them.

Badlands in the valley of the Red Deer river, north-east of Brooks. Early settlers tended to avoid them, believing they were haunted by the spirits of long-dead Indians.

Photograph Credits

Alberta Archaeological Survey: p. 8 centre and bottom; *Alberta College of Art:* p. 64 top, p. 65 top; *Alberta Culture:* p. 66 top, p. 67 top and bottom; *Alberta Government Services:* p. 4, p. 5 bottom, p. 6, p. 7 top and bottom, p. 10, p. 11 bottom, p. 14 top, p. 22 top and bottom, p. 23 top and bottom, p. 24, p. 25 top and bottom, p. 26 top and bottom, p. 27 top and bottom, p. 28, p. 29 top and bottom, p. 30, p. 31 top and bottom, p. 32 top and bottom, p. 33, p. 34, p. 35 top and bottom, p. 36 top, p. 37, p. 38 top and bottom, p. 39 top and bottom, p. 40 top and bottom, p. 42 top and bottom, p. 43 top and bottom, p. 44 top and bottom, p. 45 top and bottom, p. 47 top, p. 48, p. 49 top and bottom, p. 50 top and bottom, p. 51 top, p. 52 top, p. 53 bottom, p. 54 top and bottom, p. 55, p. 56 top and bottom, p. 57 bottom, p. 58, p. 59 top and bottom, p. 62 top and bottom, p. 63 top, p. 66 bottom, p. 68, p. 69 top and bottom, p. 70, p. 71 top and bottom, p. 72, p. 73 top and bottom, p. 74 top and bottom, p. 75 top and bottom, p. 76 top and bottom, p. 77 top and bottom, p. 78 top and bottom; *Alberta Health Sciences Centre:* p. 57 top, p. 60 top and bottom, p. 61 top and bottom; *Alberta Provincial Museum:* p. 57 top; *Robin Brass:* p. 3; *Calgary Tourist and Convention Centre:* p. 46; *City of Calgary:* p. 47 bottom, p. 68 bottom; *City of Edmonton:* p. 5 bottom; *Humphry Clinker:* p. 63 bottom; *Glenbow Museum:* p. 64 bottom; *Manitoba Archives:* p. 14 bottom; *National Map Collection:* p. 13 top; *Provincial Archives of Alberta:* p. 12, p. 13 bottom, p. 15 bottom, p. 16 bottom, p. 17 bottom, p. 21 top and bottom; *Saskatchewan Archives:* p. 19 top, p. 20 top; *Syncrude:* p. 36 bottom, p. 41 bottom, p. 52 bottom; *University of Lethbridge:* p. 41 top.

Acknowledgments

Many individuals, corporations, institutions, and government departments assisted us in gathering information and illustrations. Among them we owe special thanks to the following:

Air Canada
Alberta Agriculture
Alberta Archaeological Survey
Alberta Business Development
Alberta Construction Association
Alberta Culture
Alberta Education
Alberta Energy and Natural Resources
Alberta Environment
Alberta Executive Council
Alberta Forest Service
Alberta Game Farm
Alberta Gas Ethylene
Alberta Gas Trunk Lines
Alberta Municipal Affairs
Alberta Native Affairs
Alberta Public Affairs Bureau
Alberta Recreation, Parks and Wildlife
Alberta Transportation

Alberta Treasury
Alberta Wheat Pool
Frank Calder
Calgary Herald
Calgary Power
Calgary Tourist and Convention Centre
Canadian Cattlemen's Association
CP Rail
Canadian Petroleum Association
Canadian Rodeo Cowboys Association
Citadel Theatre
City of Calgary
City of Edmonton
City of Lethbridge
Art Clough
Coal Association of Canada
Edmonton Eskimos
Energy Resources Conservation Board
Glenbow Museum

Great Canadian Oil Sands
Vern Modine
Gina Mrklas
National Gallery of Canada
Northern Transportation
Pacific Western Airlines
Parks Canada
Provincial Museum of Alberta
Public Archives of Canada
Jo Ann Salomons
Syncrude Canada
Travel Alberta
Unifarm
University of Alberta
University of Calgary
University of Lethbridge
Alan Vanterpool

If we have unwittingly infringed copyright in any photograph reproduced in this publication, we tender our sincere apologies and will be glad of the opportunity, upon being satisfied as to the owner's title, to pay an appropriate fee as if we had been able to obtain prior permission.

Canadian Cataloguing in Publication Data

Hocking, Anthony, 1944-
   Alberta

(Canada series)

Includes index.
ISBN 0-07-082687-0

1. Alberta.   2. Alberta - Description and travel.
I. Series

FC3661.6.H63   971.23   C77-001605-7
F1076.5.H63

Index

CANADIAN STATISTICS

	Joined Confed-eration	Capital	Area	Population (1976)	Ethnic Origin (% 1971)		
					British	French	Other
CANADA		Ottawa	9 976 185 km²	22 992 604	45	29	26
Newfoundland	1949	St. John's	404 519 km²	557 725	94	3	3
Prince Edward Island	1873	Charlottetown	5 657 km²	118 229	83	14	3
Nova Scotia	1867	Halifax	55 491 km²	828 571	77	10	13
New Brunswick	1867	Fredericton	74 437 km²	677 250	58	37	5
Quebec	1867	Quebec City	1 540 687 km²	6 234 445	11	79	10
Ontario	1867	Toronto	1 068 587 km²	8 264 465	59	10	31
Manitoba	1870	Winnipeg	650 090 km²	1 021 506	42	9	49
Saskatchewan	1905	Regina	651 903 km²	921 323	42	6	52
Alberta	1905	Edmonton	661 188 km²	1 838 037	47	6	47
British Columbia	1871	Victoria	948 600 km²	2 466 608	58	4	38
Yukon	—	Whitehorse	536 327 km²	21 836	49	7	56
Northwest Territories	—	Yellowknife	3 379 699 km²	42 609	25	7	68